Praise for *Out o*

"I'm very excited for people looking to do transformational work with the Enneagram to get their hands on this book. Associating the Enneatypes with elemental archetypal expressions, the reader is aided in moving beyond stereotypical descriptions into articulating more expansive parts of the human experience often less accessible in other Enneagram material. Drawing on how beautiful images and stunning symbolism tend to speak more powerfully without words, this book will awaken potential and evoke deeper kinds of inner work. Stephanie has put together something new for the Ennea-world that's quite beautiful, awe inspiring, and very accessible."
- **Seth Abram**, founder of *Integrated Enneagram*, and co-host of the Enneagram podcast, *Fathoms*

"An important book for getting us Enneagram students out of our heads and back into nature. The Enneagram was never meant to be exclusively about our own self-knowledge and interpersonal relationships, but to ground us firmly and decisively in the more-than-human world. Through imagery and inquiry, *Out of the Box & Into the Wild* speaks to the truth that humans are profoundly wild beings that evolved in rhythm with the turning of the Earth and the cycles of the moon, alongside crashing waves and howling wolves. I hope that it is the first of many Enneagram books that accounts for our wild nature."
- **Ben Campbell**, founder of *Wild Enneagram*

"*Out of The Box & Into the Wild* is a creative approach to the Enneagram you aren't going to want to miss. Using the elements of nature to relate to the types and the triads makes for a fascinating approach to self-exploration and a beautiful reminder that we are all connected."
- **Sarajane Case**, author of *The Enneagram Letters*

"This is the Enneagram book I've been waiting for! Spencer gives us invaluable insight, metaphor, and images in the study of our personality types. I will be coming back to this book again and again!"
- **Scott Erickson**, author of *Honest Advent* and *Say Yes*

"This must-read guide on the Enneagram Triadic groups contains everything you need to know if you want to understand the Enneagram types with an embodied and emotional depth. The use of nature imagery and metaphor moves beyond dry descriptions of personalities and cuts straight to the heart."
- **Chelsea Forbrook**, Enneagram Educator, Spiritual Director, and author of *Blessing My Demons: How to Name, Tame, and Transform Your Inner Critic*

"Spencer is one of those exemplary Enneagram writers who can combine thorough knowledge with heart-opening creativity. Using the wisdom of the earth itself, this book will absolutely change the way you see both yourself and the Enneagram. This is unlike any Enneagram book you have ever read."
- **Rev. Phil GebbenGreen**, Presbyterian Pastor and Enneagram Prison Project faculty member

"In this captivating new addition to our Enneagram library, Stephanie weaves poetic writing into memorable prose, along with beautiful graphics to illuminate every key concept. *Out of the Box & Into the Wild* is both an introduction to the Enneagram and the 9 types and also an exploration of the most important Triads inherent in the Enneagram. Whether you are new to Enneagram and like breadth and depth or if you are already Enneagram savvy and want to go deeper, you'll want to read this book."
- **Ginger Lapid-Bogda PhD**, past-president of the International Enneagram Association and author of *Bringing Out the Best in Yourself at Work*, *The Art of Typing*, and *Transform Your Team with the Enneagram*

"*Out of the Box & Into the Wild* is a poignant and beautiful addition to Enneagram literature, filled with moving imagery and grounding explanations of the Triads. As a Type 5 and an artist, I felt my heart squeeze viewing Spencer's gorgeous imagery and enjoying the way she masterfully weaves design into a deeper knowledge of this tool. I'd recommend this book to anyone who wants a more nuanced and mystical experience learning about the Enneagram."
- **Melissa Kircher**, Enneagram Coach and curator of the account @enneagrampaths

"This book is a must have for everyone who is using the Enneagram on their journey to wholeness. It provides an insightful and transformational path to our individual depths in the exciting language of symbols. Stephanie's creative, original use of images from nature are helping me to go deeper into the Enneagram Triads, use them in a more powerful way, and become more aware of my inner and outer worlds. The images continue to nourish my body and soul. I whole-heartedly recommend this book."
- **Anne Mureé**, Enneagram Educator and Transformational Enneagram Coach

"*Out of the Box & Into the Wild* gives us a novel metaphor to imagine the Enneagram styles and centers. Illustrating the psychological world with the physical world creates an intriguing synthesis. In the spirit of art, it helps us see things from a different perspective, another lens for viewing the Enneagram. This Journey will spark the reader's own imagination and understanding."
- **Jerome Wagner PhD**, Honorary IEA Founder

OUT OF THE BOX & INTO THE WILD

An Enneagram Journey
Through the Triads of Nature

STEPHANIE J SPENCER

PUNCHLINE
PUBLISHERS

Copyright © 2023 by Stephanie J Spencer

All rights reserved. No part of this book
may be reproduced or used in any manner
without written permission of the copyright owner
except for the use of quotations in a book review.

First Edition June 2023

ISBN
Softcover: 978-1-955051-19-4
Hardcover: 978-1-955051-21-7
eBook:978-1-955051-20-0

Published by Punchline Publishers
www.punchlineagency.com

www.stephaniejspencer.com
@beyondyournumber

In gratitude for my family,
who supported and cheered me on through the long hours
and work of pulling this book together.

In dedication to my coaching clients,
who teach me how to help people get out of boxes
by sharing their personal stories of growth and change.

"Everybody needs beauty as well as bread, places to play in and pray in, where nature may heal and give strength to body and soul alike."

John Muir

Table of Contents

Introduction — 1
My Enneagram Story — 1
Why this Book — 4
Overview of the Enneagram — 6
How to Use this Book — 10

How We Perceive & Process the World: Elements & the Intelligence Center Triads — 11
Earth & the Gut Center Triad: Types 8, 9, and 1 — 14
Water & the Heart Center Triad: Types 2, 3, and 4 — 22
Air & the Head Center Triad: Types 5, 6, and 7 — 30

How We Move & Get Needs Met in the World: Climate Zones & the Energy Triads — 39
The Tropical Zone & the Active Energy Triad: Types 8, 3, and 7 — 42
The Boreal Zone & the Receptive Energy Triad: Types 9, 4, and 5 — 50
The Temperate Zone & the Balancing Energy Triad: Types 1, 2, and 6 — 58

How We React to & Cope with the World: Animal Groupings & the Harmonic Triads — 67
Carnivores & the Reactivity Triad: Types 8, 4, and 6 — 70
Herbivores & the Positivity Triad: Types 9, 2, and 7 — 78
Omnivores & the Competency Triad: Types 1, 3, and 5 — 86

How We Relate to & Provide for the World: Plant Groupings & the Collaboration Triads — 95
Spore-producing Plants & the Relationalist Triad: Types 8, 2, and 5 — 98
Rhizome-making Plants & the Pragmatist Triad: Types 9, 6, and 3 — 106
Flower-bearing Plants & the Idealist Triad: Types 1, 4, and 7 — 114

Conclusion — 123
Pulling It All Together — 123
Collage Images — 124
Closing Reflection — 143

Appendices — 144
Traditional Enneagram Terminology — 144
Recommended Resources — 145
Photo Credits — 146
Scientific Information Sources — 147
Acknowledgments — 149

"What a long time it can take to become the person one has always been! How often in the process we mask ourselves in faces that are not our own. How much dissolving and shaking of ego we must endure before we discover our deep identity—the true self within every human being that is the seed of authentic vocation."

Parker Palmer

Introduction

My Enneagram Story

My journey with the Enneagram has been long and layered. I find this is true for many of us who have experienced the Enneagram. We tend to think about finding our Enneagram Type as a quick test and answer. When, in reality, knowing our Type and what to do with that information takes a lifetime of learning.

In 2015, I attended Dr. Jerry Wagner's Enneagram Spectrum Training. Dr. Wagner began that training by handing out binders of information that began with bibliographies about where to find more information. Suddenly, he laughed and reminded us he was an Enneagram Type 5, saying, *"It's important to know the Enneagram Type of your Enneagram teachers."*

I've come back to this moment time and again over the years. Understanding knowledge and competency as high priorities of Type 5s, my defenses came down as he handed out those binders. I was more open to learning from Dr. Wagner's perspective without feeling intimidated by the quantity of information in his teaching. Laughing together about the ways our Types show up in all we do allowed me to be more present to his teaching.

The Enneagram System will be explained in the following pages. But, first, I want to follow Dr. Wagner's wisdom, and begin with telling you my Enneagram Type and the journey it was for me to discover it. My Enneagram Type brings both insight and blindspots to my approach and perspective to the Enneagram system.

Prior to Dr. Wagner's training, I had learned about the Enneagram from my spiritual director. She and I were processing how I did not feel seen or valued in a leadership position. I was spiraling as I wondered who I really was as a person— both inside and outside my job. As she explained the Enneagram, I fell in love (even before I knew my type). Enneagram helped me see I was both unique and not alone. There were reasons why I was doing what I was doing and feeling the way I was feeling. Most importantly, there was a system to describe who I was (without putting me in a box) and pathways toward growth and healing.

After much exploration in books and CDs (yes, these were the days of people circulating audio recordings of old workshops that had been ripped to CDs), I initially thought I was a Type 3 but eventually landed on being an Enneagram Type 2.

There were definitely Type 2 patterns in my life. I could see ways I spent my energy helping others in order to avoid addressing aspects of myself. Up until that point, I had been a pastor so it was my literal job to care for people. As I looked more deeply into the motivations for playing the "helper" role, I realized I had some hard work to do, especially in opening to my own heart.

That's when I decided to travel to Chicago for Dr. Wagner's Enneagram Spectrum training, which was an incredible chance to learn more about the Enneagram System

and its Types. Dr. Wagner talked about how Enneagram work was like peeling back the layers of an onion in our psyche, and that's how it felt. Seeing myself as a Type 2 was giving me language and a framework to create better boundaries and examine my own feelings. I wanted to help others do the same; so after returning from that training, I began work as an Enneagram coach.

The journey was difficult but rewarding. And after a few more years of inner work and coaching, I realized a complicated truth: I was not an Enneagram Type 2.

I had seen myself as a Type 2 because I recognized the ways I was focusing on others and avoiding things I needed. But facing my own needs made me realize Type 2's deeper motivations did not actually fit me. But what was I supposed to do with this new insight? It seemed awkward to change Types publicly, especially after coaching others! I thought for a second about ignoring what I was seeing, but I knew I had to be honest.

Though embarrassing at first, I have come to see my initial "mis-Typing" as an important part of my Enneagram journey. It was the necessary work of peeling back the layers of my identity and motivations. I had to do healing work on the outer layer before I could see what was happening at a deeper level. Approaches to the Enneagram too often focus on getting our Type "right." This can put us in a box where we miss the potential for growth.

Once I could see I was not a Type 2, it was time to look at all the Types again (including ones I had previously closed off). I had never really considered Type 4, since none of the stereotypical Type 4 descriptions fit me. No one would describe me as someone who "rides the waves of emotion" in a group. I didn't see myself as "melancholy" or "envious." But one day, I was listening to a podcast episode in which someone used the word "longing" instead of "envy" to describe Type 4s, and I found myself nodding along to the entire conversation. Sometimes changing one word can change everything.

I opened to the possibility of being a Type 4, and dove back into the work of Beatrice Chestnut, PhD, who describes the three versions of each Type in relation to the instinctual subtype layer of the Enneagram (more on this later). I had a sudden clarity, and wondered how I missed it for so long. I was a Type 4. More specifically, I was (and still am) a Self-Preservation* Type 4.

In hindsight, my difficulty in seeing I was a Self-Preservation Type 4 makes sense. Having a self-preservation dominant instinct (or subtype) means I want to be safe; I spend a lot of internal energy preserving my sense of security. So even though I have all the emotions of a Type 4, I tend to hide my feelings, making the melancholy harder to spot. Furthermore, an "envious" self-preservation energizes me to achieve what others have, which looks less like a Type 4 and more like a Type 3. Except that it carries the twist of making the work harder than it needs to be and "suffering" as a result. (Fun!) Finally, since I was introduced to Enneagram in a time of struggle, transition, and stress, I was spiraling, and not operating as my core self. Enneagram Types have a tendency to move into the behaviors of another Type in stress, and for Type 4, that movement takes me to Type 2, which is likely why I identified so deeply with that Type.

Why am I sharing all this with you?

First, because I hope my Enneagram journey is a reminder to be gentle and patient in the Typing process and beyond. The Enneagram is not meant to be reduced to a simple test that puts us in boxes. We are humans with layers of stories, fears, and desires that take time, even years, to peel back. Add the complexity from our instinctual subtypes, and many of us require more time and exploration than a simple assessment provides. As you read this book, I encourage you to remain open to seeing something you've perhaps never seen before.

Second, because of Dr. Wagner's wisdom, *"It's important to know the Enneagram Type of your Enneagram teachers."* I want you to know that being a Type 4 will affect my perspective in this book.

In fact, I am giggling right now about how my Type is already showing, since I have chosen to start this book by sharing the nuances of my own story. As a Type 4, I tend to focus on the uniqueness and depth of our individual human experiences. Experiencing life through emotion and complexity, as Type 4s often do, gives me a resistance to generalizations and an appreciation for the ways descriptions, lists, and words have limits. This means I have always drifted towards describing life through metaphor, sometimes to the point of overuse. Combining that with the ways Type 4s seek beauty and use creativity to reveal inner worlds, birthing the imagery in this book has felt like a natural outflow of who I am. As a Type that is both in the Heart Center Triad and Receptive Triad (more on those Triads later), I have created a work designed to increase our compassion towards ourselves and each other, while offering a spaciousness to explore without being pushed in too specific of a direction.

My hope for you as you move through the content of this book is that you give yourself the space to wonder. Use my personal story as a point of reflection as you consider your own Enneagram Type. Allow the images to open your imagination to see more than you have seen before. Notice how the Triads are at work around you, bringing both connection and uniqueness to how you are experiencing the world. Peel back the layers of who you are.

Jump *out of the box & into the wild.*
- Stephanie J Spencer

---

* *Instinctual Subtype study is a layer of the Enneagram that examines how the primal force of one of three biological drives (self-preservation, social, and one-to-one or sexual) combines with our Enneagram Type to forge three different versions of each Type. The nuances of these 27 subtype variations is an extremely valuable exploration, but is also beyond the scope of this work. If you want to learn more about Instinctual Subtypes, I encourage you to go to cpenneagram.com. Beatrice Chestnut and Uranio Paes are experts and guides who dive into this layer of the Enneagram with both wisdom and heart.*

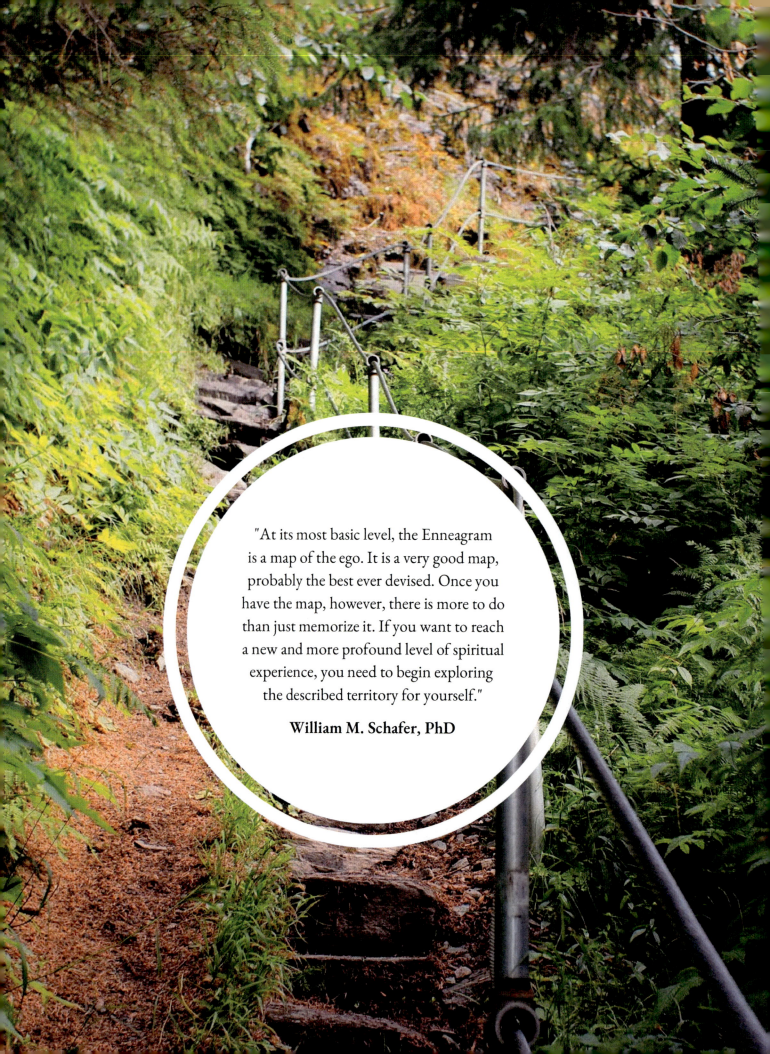

"At its most basic level, the Enneagram is a map of the ego. It is a very good map, probably the best ever devised. Once you have the map, however, there is more to do than just memorize it. If you want to reach a new and more profound level of spiritual experience, you need to begin exploring the described territory for yourself."

William M. Schafer, PhD

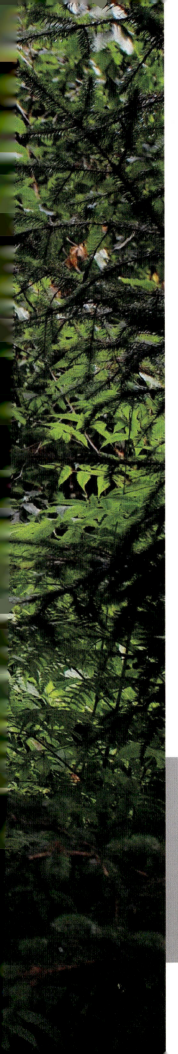

Why this Book

I fell in love with the Enneagram all those years ago because of its unmatched ability to help humans understand ourselves and each other. It is a tool that is both clarifying and complex, bringing language to our identities and motivations, offering us both uniqueness and a sense of belonging.

A foundational Triad grouping of Enneagram is that of the Intelligence Centers: the *head*, *heart*, and *gut*. All three Intelligence Center Triads are important, yet many of us have only experienced Enneagram content through the *head* in an information-based and analytic approach.

This Head Center Triad approach is informative but limited. If we aren't careful, reading too many Enneagram Type descriptions can become more like boxes than pathways for growth. Not only that, sometimes words can trigger our defense mechanisms and close us off, as represented in my Enneagram story. In my work with coaching clients, I have noticed the ways imagery can soften those defense mechanisms and help us see the Enneagram, and ourselves, differently.

This book is meant to help you travel *out of the box* and *into the wild*, using natural imagery. The images tell the story of the Enneagram in layers, first describing one of the Triads, then how each Type can be represented within that Triad. As you read, this imagery will first engage your heart, moving beyond intellectual barriers as you open to beauty. Then, it will engage your gut as you (hopefully) walk through the world experiencing your embodied connection to everyone and everything around you.

> *Any book using the Enneagram rests on the shoulders of past teachers.*
> *The insights of George Gurdjieff, Oscar Ichazo, Claudio Naranjo, Helen Palmer, David Daniels, Don Riso, Russ Hudson, Jerry Wagner, Ginger Lapid-Bogda, Beatrice Chestnut, Uranio Paes, and more have formed the Enneagram into the rich wisdom tool it is today. There are many great Enneagram teachers past and present who have taught me what I know. The Type and Triad descriptions in this book are in my own words as much as possible, but they originate with the aforementioned teachers. Please use this book alongside their work. See the Appendix for recommended resources and traditional Enneagram terminology.*

Overview of the Enneagram

The Enneagram Symbol

The Enneagram Symbol is a visual picture of the energy and interaction of the Types. The circle reminds us we are all connected.

To some extent, we each hold and display all nine Types. However, we rest in one number as our core Type. Our Enneagram Type is the primary lens through which we experience the world. When we know our Type, we uncover and explore what we are afraid of, what we desire, and what makes us feel vulnerable. Knowing our Enneagram Type helps us name our shadows with compassion and take steps to live more deeply into our gifts.

Enneagram Types connected to our core Type by arrow lines reflect our tendency to energetically "move" in different circumstances. In times of stress, we tend to be "pulled" with the arrow, compelled toward behaving like the Type at the end of that arrow line. In relaxed or secure states, we tend to let our guard down and open to the energy of the Type at the end of the arrow line pointing towards our Type. Like our core Type, the Enneagram Types at the end of our arrow lines are important parts of who we are. In fact, learning to integrate those two Types in times other than stress and security is a key component of moving forward in wholeness.

The Enneagram Triads

When we remove the inner arrow lines, there is space to draw inner triangles that divide the 9 Types into four distinct Triads. These Triads describe ways that we interact with the world, revealing places of both tension and connection. Through the Triads, all Enneagram Types have at least one place of commonality with each of the other Types.

The Intelligence Center Triads describe how we perceive and process the world. Types 8, 9, and 1 are in the Gut Center Triad, Types 2, 3, and 4 are in the Heart Center Triad, and Types 5, 6, and 7 are in the Head Center Triad.

The Energy Triads (otherwise known as Hornevian Groups or Social Stances) describe how we move and get needs met in the world. Types 8, 3, and 7 are in the Active Energy Triad, Types 9, 4, and 5 are in the Receptive Energy Triad, and Types 1, 2, and 6 are in the Balancing Energy Triad.

The Harmonic Triads describe how we react to and cope with the world. Types 8, 4, and 6 are in the Reactivity Triad, Types 9, 2, and 7 are in the Positivity Triad, and Types 1, 3, and 5 are in the Competency Triad.

The Collaboration Triads (otherwise known as Harmony Triads or Object Relation Triads) describe how we relate to and provide for the world. Types 8, 2, and 5 are in the Relationalist Triad, Types 9, 3, and 6 are in the Pragmatist Triad, and Types 1, 4, and 7 are in the Idealist Triad.

Priorities: excellence, goodness
Struggles: resentment, criticalness
Strengths: reliability, wisdom, commitment, objectivity
Characteristics: focused, correcting, advocating, reasoning, simplifying

Priorities: connection, love
Struggles: pride, manipulation
Strengths: compassion, intuition, hospitality, empathy
Characteristics: rescuing, serving, listening, accepting, networking

Priorities: worth, achievement
Struggles: vanity, deception
Strengths: charm, productivity, efficiency, team-orientation
Characteristics: strategic, dynamic, impatient, performing, motivating

Priorities: identity, depth
Struggles: longing, melancholy
Strengths: sensitivity, expression, creativity, emotional honesty
Characteristics: romantic, nostalgic, artistic, spiritual, unique

The Enneagram Types

No Enneagram Type is better or worse than another. This is why numbers are more helpful. As soon as we add words, we have feelings about what we do and don't want to be. All nine Types carry important facets of what it means to be human.

Enneagram Type 1s have the ability to see what *could* be. Whether that vision is for a room, a project, or the world, they carry both the idealism and responsibility to make things better. But because things are not as they could be, for Type 1s, the possibility of *could* often shifts to the weight of *should*. They become critical of ways things fall short of their (high) expectations. This can lead Type 1s to become perfectionistic about the things that are most important to their inner sense of what is right or good. Type 1s struggle with anger and resentment about all that is not right, even while they keep up the behaviors of what a "good person" looks like.

Enneagram Type 2s are naturally good at filling needs. They have a desire to help and an instinctual ability to plug into places that make a difference to teams, projects, and people. This can develop into a need to be needed and a thirst to be indispensable. Type 2s have a deep desire to be loved, but can begin to feel like they are cared about not because of who they are but because of what they do for others. This traps them in a string of imbalanced relationships, where they give, but do not receive. This is why their struggle is pride; Type 2s forget they are human and have needs like everyone else.

Enneagram Type 3s have a natural ability to be successful. Their instincts guide them toward what will create a positive image and achieve their goals in a variety of situations. Type 3s are motivated towards productivity and achievement, driven by a desire to feel valuable and accepted. Their success can serve as a trap, however, as their self image becomes based on how they perform and produce. When that happens, Type 3s can become status-conscious, and focused on image. They struggle with deceiving both themselves and others, as they show not who they really are, but who they think others want to see.

Enneagram Type 4s want to find and express depth and meaning. They are driven to actualize the significance of their identity, which leads to quests for beauty, individualism, and authentic emotional expression. Often, Type 4s choose non-traditional paths such as the arts or spirituality as they seek to be known as their unique and fullest selves. This desire is a trap that can leave them stuck in longing and envy, as they feel misunderstood and over-connect to what is missing in their lives. All this leads Type 4s to struggle with feelings of melancholy and disenchantment with the ordinary.

Enneagram Type 5s are independent and observant learners of the world. They are often wise and perceptive thinkers who want to be capable and competent before taking action. Type 5s are able to view situations from a perspective that allows them to analyze, synthesize, and understand. This can lead them to an exaggerated need to know and figure things out. When that happens, they become more compartmentalizing and intellectual. Type 5s can struggle with becoming detached from both their presence and feelings as they escape into their heads. They retreat to guard information, energy, and privacy.

Enneagram Type 6s are good at putting together puzzles. Whether a family, system, or project, they can see how all the pieces fit together, and want to keep everything in place. They are reliable, trustworthy, and hard working. Their ability and desire to see how things fit can also lead to a focus on what doesn't fit or could go wrong. Type 6s want to feel secure. Their brains can get sucked into holding the domino effects of choices. In response to the fear that arises from this way of thinking, 6s may be compelled to avoid, plan for, or conquer the foreshadowed catastrophes.

Enneagram Type 7s carry a natural enthusiasm and zest for life. They look for adventures to keep life interesting. This pursuit of pleasure can be a fun and spontaneous energy that spills out to those around them. However, this energy can also turn into an avoidance of slowing down. Type 7s fear being trapped in pain or boredom. Hunger for more becomes a way to escape feelings of emptiness. They can be scattered and undisciplined as they stretch themselves too thin across all their interests. The fear of missing out can keep Type 7s from being present to what is in front of them.

Enneagram Type 8s intuitively sense where power resides in others and in themselves. They are assertive and decisive challengers. Strong and independent, Type 8s have a desire to push for justice and protect the vulnerable. This energy can sometimes lean towards being proud, domineering, or confrontational when they push too hard or protect too much. They value self-reliance and can have an exaggerated need to be in control. Type 8s struggle with a conquering drive to move and acquire.

Enneagram Type 9s desire harmony. They are easygoing and mediating, as they see the world from multiple perspectives. They want to go with the flow, and provide a supportive presence to those around them. However, their hope for harmony can result in Type 9s avoiding conflict instead of creating peace, as they substitute comfort for understanding. They can become complacent and passive, settling for what they get. Their fear of separation and tendency toward resignation can combine and cause Type 9s to merge with others and lose their own identity.

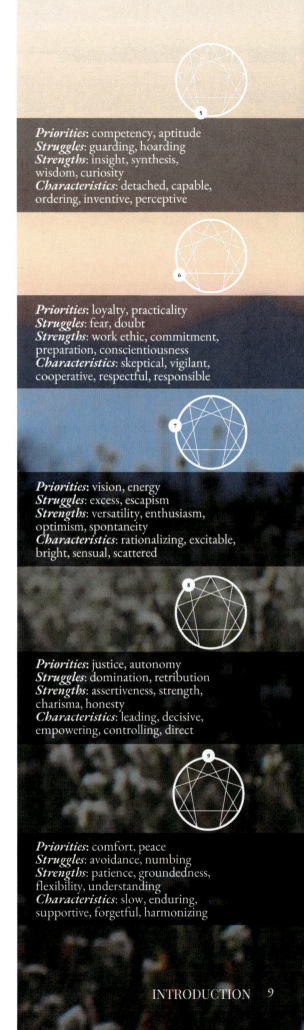

Priorities: competency, aptitude
Struggles: guarding, hoarding
Strengths: insight, synthesis, wisdom, curiosity
Characteristics: detached, capable, ordering, inventive, perceptive

Priorities: loyalty, practicality
Struggles: fear, doubt
Strengths: work ethic, commitment, preparation, conscientiousness
Characteristics: skeptical, vigilant, cooperative, respectful, responsible

Priorities: vision, energy
Struggles: excess, escapism
Strengths: versatility, enthusiasm, optimism, spontaneity
Characteristics: rationalizing, excitable, bright, sensual, scattered

Priorities: justice, autonomy
Struggles: domination, retribution
Strengths: assertiveness, strength, charisma, honesty
Characteristics: leading, decisive, empowering, controlling, direct

Priorities: comfort, peace
Struggles: avoidance, numbing
Strengths: patience, groundedness, flexibility, understanding
Characteristics: slow, enduring, supportive, forgetful, harmonizing

INTRODUCTION

How to Use this Book

Allow this book to open you up to new possibilities.

If you do not already know your Enneagram Type, as you read, create space for reflection on these images. Allow them to be a discernment tool.
What Type speaks to you?
Which priorities resonate with you?
What kinds of struggles have you experienced?
What kinds of strengths have you demonstrated?
Which characteristics feel most like you?

If you do know your Enneagram Type, meditate on the images for your Type and its Triads.
What is beautiful about your Type that you haven't noticed before?
How does it feel to be symbolically connected to other Types in your Triads?
Which image speaks to you the most? Why?

Whether you do or do not know your Type, be curious about all the images and Types.
Is there something you have in common with other Types that you haven't noticed before?
If you tend to struggle with certain Types (as we all do!), is there something in the Triads or imagery that brings a new level of compassion or understanding?

Allow the images in this book to reside in your imagination as you walk about your daily life.
Embody them where you live as you spend time in the nature around you.
Is there an image you can encounter on a regular basis that speaks to you about your Type?
How can you get out of the box and into the wild where you live?

Open your heart. Let the beauty of the earth speak and hear what it has to say.

How We Perceive & Process the World:
Elements & the Intelligence Center Triads

As ancient civilizations studied the material world, they saw the major elements of earth, water, and air. These, along with fire, were seen as the essence by which everything else arose. Science has since moved its understanding of substance to concepts such as the periodic table or states of matter but that does not mean we have to abandon this wisdom from the Ancients.

Earth provides reliable grounding. Because of its stability, seeds can grow and beings can move. Water provides the nourishment needed for life to flourish. It is the flowing vitality that connects every organism to one another. Air provides substance to breathe. It is the open expanse into which things can grow and from which they receive.

All three of these elements are important for the world and each element is distinct in function from one another. In the Enneagram system, the nine Types are divided into three distinct Intelligence Center Triads through which we perceive and process the world.

Types 8, 9, and 1 are in the Gut Center Triad. Types in this Triad ask, "What does my instinct tell me is true?" Their decisions are based on things like comfort, independence, and energy, which means they can get caught in the struggle of anger as they guard their autonomy. They strive for control by protecting themselves (Type 8), staying comfortable (Type 9), or being right (Type 1). Their communication style tends to be direct, plain, sometimes defensive, and full of nonverbal cues. At their best, these Types process with serenity and strength.

Types 2, 3, and 4 are in the Heart Center Triad. Types in this Triad ask, "How does this affect my connection to self and others?" Their decisions are based on things like relationships, image, and emotion, which means they can get caught in the struggle of shame as they look for self-worth. They strive for identity by being liked (Type 2), feeling valuable (Type 3), or finding significance (Type 4). Their communication style tends to contain stories, metaphor, and implied or unspoken meaning. At their best, these Types process with authenticity and compassion.

Types 5, 6, and 7 are in the Head Center Triad. Types in this Triad ask, "How can I prepare myself and those around me?" Their decisions are based on things like logic, security, and planning, which means they can get caught in the struggle of fear as they search for support. They strive for safety by being competent (Type 5), having support (Type 6), or not being restricted (Type 7). Their communication style tends to be analytical, thoughtful, and sometimes complicated. At their best, these Types process with clarity and guidance.

The Gut Center Triad is like earth, the Heart Center Triad is like water, and the Head Center Triad is like air. Think about how different the world would be if any one of the elements of earth, water, or air were missing. The same is true for humanity. These three different ways of perceiving and processing the world are each valuable. Each Triad offers something important for the flourishing of humanity.

Earth & The Gut Center Triad
Enneagram Types 8, 9, & 1

Earth takes up space. Boulders, sand, and peat. Mountains, hills, and plains. All these components define landscapes. In every place in the world, it is earth that provides ground for seeds to land, be held and nourished, and burst into life.

Though earth holds space for the transformation of seeds and landscapes, earth itself is not easily changed. Dirt can be watered until it becomes mud. Rocks can be worn down until they become sand. Yet, in the midst of these shifts, there is something fundamental that remains autonomous and steady. The makeup of earth itself does not transform. It is still dirt and rock.

Earth's resistance makes it powerful, which can sometimes make it both a barrier and a substance of protection. It is the primary element used to create safe dwellings for living things.

For all humans, earth, quite literally, is the grounded place on which we stand.

The Types in the Gut Center can change the landscape of rooms with the way they carry their presence. Others are often comforted by the grounded strength and stability Gut Types carry as they filter and process through body and instinct. In that way of processing, Gut Types work to guard their autonomy, which can bring a stubborn resistance if they feel forced to move. The way they focus on the simple needs of the moment gives these Types an uncomplicated presence that can feel spacious to others.

- *Priorities*: comfort, instinct, energy, autonomy
- *Struggles*: anger and control
- *Strengths*: serenity, strength, groundedness
- *Characteristics*: protecting, resisting, empowering, simplifying

Reflection Questions for Types in the Gut Center Triad:
Have others experienced me as a grounding presence? When? How?
How do I take up space in the world? Do I sense the magnitude of my presence?
When have I resisted change? How did that affect me?

Rock
Enneagram Type 8

Rocks are solid. They form the outer crust of the earth, providing the base on which existence depends. They are strong enough to be walked on, built on, and climbed upon. Whether small river stones or large mountain boulders, rocks have a density and form that does not crumble easily. Rocks are seen and their impact is felt. This world is sometimes classified as "the third rock from the sun." It is rock that helps this planet hold its shape and maintain its orbit.

That does not, however, make rock impervious. It can be carved into canyons by rivers and broken into pieces by earthquakes. Miners can drill into it to excavate its metal content and sculptors can shape it into a new form.

Ultimately, rock is not the singular tough substance it appears to be. A rock is a collection of minerals that bond through environmental pressure. New rocks are formed when magma cools, sediments compact, or existing rocks are compressed. Rocks have a complex and difficult history that has created their current state of existence.

Occasionally, this pressure creates gems of striking beauty. Rubies, sapphires, amethysts, diamonds— all these are rocks that have become some of the world's most treasured goods. Gems are rocks that have to submit to mining, refining, cutting, and polishing for their inner brilliance to truly shine.

Rock creates a strong foundation from which mutual flourishing is possible.

Type 8s tend to have an unshakeable strength. They make an impact on situations because of the way they enter with confident presence. That toughness can sometimes cause Type 8s to dominate others and hide their vulnerability. When Type 8s learn to expose their vulnerability, even to the point of being cut and refined, their true brilliance and beauty is revealed. When healthy, Type 8s bring a just and firm foundation from which the rest of humanity can be empowered to flourish.

Reflection questions for Type 8s:
How do I experience my strength? How can I get in touch with my vulnerability?
Do I believe that I could carry the beauty and value of a precious gem? Why or why not?
Are others experiencing my presence as weighty? How is that affecting their actions?

9

Soil
Enneagram Type 9

Soil is a yielding and nutrient-rich dirt. It holds a vast mixture of elements including organic material, gas, water, and living creatures. This composition creates a unified substance perfect for supporting the growth of its co-habitants.

Entire ecosystems are dependent upon the health of soil. It regulates water quality, provides a habitat for biodiverse microorganisms, and processes carbon back into the atmosphere. It provides an aerated environment for the oxygenation of plants and processes diseases and contaminants to be less toxic. Soil is essential, and yet, in its unassuming and often hidden state, it can easily be taken for granted. Conscious cultivation and fertilization helps soil, and everything around it, become healthier.

Soil is layered. The deeper into the earth it is, the denser it becomes. At the top, there is a porous and nourishing layer, able to receive water with space for roots to move and grow. However, deeper below, there is a solid and stubborn layer that both roots and humans can sometimes find impenetrable.

Soil is formed as it receives a conglomeration of substances that affect each other over time. It creates a feedback loop where the organic material left behind from the plants it nourished becomes part of what it offers to the next set of plants. At the same time, it is not the same substance as those plants. Soil carries an important identity that is more than the sum of its parts.

When it is tended, soil becomes the key to the generativity of its environment.

Type 9s tend to have an easy and supportive presence. They carry a little bit of everything inside of them, and that resonance is felt by those around them. That conglomeration that helps others grow can sometimes cause Type 9s to both merge with the priorities of those around them and bring resistance when those priorities hit too deeply. When Type 9s learn to consciously cultivate the importance of their own presence, the truth of their essentiality is felt more deeply by those around them. When healthy, Type 9s nurture the productivity of their ecosystems.

Reflection Questions for Type 9s:
Where am I creating spaces for others to grow? Where am I yielding more than needed?
How do I hold a mix of others in the substance of who I am? Do I see my own identity?
When has my resistance created good boundaries? When have I been stubborn?

1

Clay
Enneagram Type 1

Clay is dense and heavy. This makes it a strong material that is resistant to erosion. It is made up of unique minerals, formed when rocks come into contact with water or steam. Clay minerals are usually white when they are pure, but clay itself is often brown or red due to the presence of iron oxide.

When wet, clay is moldable because of the way its fine grain particles evenly bond to water particles. This means clay is not a good material for plants as its density makes it hard to penetrate, and its particles absorb the water the plants need. On the other hand, these same features set clay apart, allowing both lovely and useful objects to be shaped from it.

If clay dries slowly, it can become rigid, cracked, or fragile. This happens particularly when the particles are so small and tight that water gets trapped and cannot evaporate evenly. However, when put in fire, the water in clay hyper-evaporates, and the minerals bind to each other, causing the clay to become hard and strong. The ability of clay to hold its shape when exposed to high heat is unique.

Because of this, clay has been useful and important in the development of humanity. The first known writing devices were clay tablets. Pottery was forged from clay, which opened the door to the subsequent advances of beer and wine-making. Perhaps most importantly, clay has been used to make bricks, which created structures and cities that couldn't have been imagined without its properties. Creators, from sculptors to potters, have depended upon clay to form stunning works of art.

Clay has played an essential role in advancing societies and sculpting beauty.

Type 1s tend to have a solid presence, valuing practicality and structure. They reach for the value of lasting durability. Since Type 1s resist being cracked in the process of change, people may be frustrated or confused by the dense impenetrability they encounter in Type 1s. When Type 1s submit to being transformed, shaped, and fired, their true purpose is recognized. When healthy, Type 1s bring a combination of usefulness and beauty to society that helps all of us reach for something greater.

Reflection Questions for Type 1s:
How are others experiencing me? Where am I coming across as impenetrable?
When have others reached greater heights because of what I provided?
Do I sense the inner purity innate in my presence? Where am I still working to achieve that perfection through my efforts?

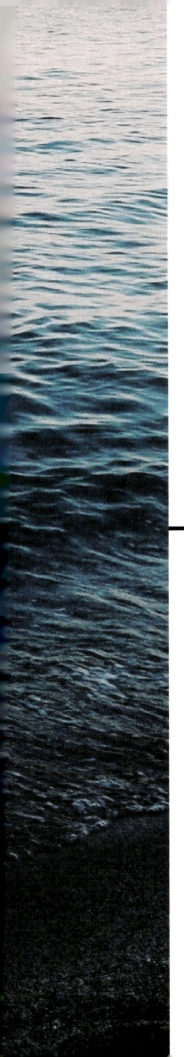

Water & The Heart Center Triad
Enneagram Types 2, 3, & 4

All known forms of life depend on one thing: water. Humans can survive up to three weeks without food, but only up to three days without water. It is used in almost every process of the human body, from delivering oxygen to processing toxins, from regulating temperature to creating brain cells. For humans, water is our primary source of well-being.

Water changes its shape in response to environmental factors, existing in forms of solid, liquid, and gas. In liquid form it is shape shifting, adjusting to fill whatever space it occupies. Yet, even though water conforms, it also influences. Water can sometimes be held back with a barricade, but it is often able to meander over, around, and through whatever is in its way. Given enough time, the flow of water has enough power to shape rock into canyons.

Whether lake, river, or ocean, the waters of the earth are teeming with life, both in and around them. Water provides habitat, transportation, and nourishment for an abundant variety of organisms. It is a generous source of good. At the same time, water can dry up or become scarce if not managed well. It can also become polluted with toxins if not guarded.

Water is a precious resource central to the nourishment of the world.

The Types in the Heart Center are sensitive to how their movements affect others. Heart Types can nourish those around them, bringing a sensitive presence as they process their environment through emotion and connection. As they do so, Heart Types are working to form their identity. This can cause them to dry up or feel corrupted if they aren't careful with their own hearts. They can have more influence than they realize because of how they shape things over time. The compassion and emotional awareness of Heart Types can provide for the welfare of those in and around their circle.

- *Priorities*: identity, emotion, relationship, image
- *Struggles*: sadness and shame
- *Strengths*: authenticity, compassion, creativity
- *Characteristics*: praising, empathizing, connecting, feeling

Reflection Questions for Types in the Heart Center Triad:
How do I carry nurturing sensitivity into the environment around me?
When have communities changed shape because of my influence?
When have I mismanaged the resource of my presence and lost track of who I am?

HOW WE PERCEIVE & PROCESS THE WORLD

River
Enneagram Type 2

Since ancient times, humans have found provision near rivers. From washing to fishing to transportation, rivers have been the center of existence for societies for thousands of years. They also serve as natural boundaries.

Rivers flow into and through terrains and change them. They bring nourishment, create places of growth, and offer passage. When they move hard and fast, they can slice gorges into once smooth ground. Rivers move in one direction, while also being responsive to their environments. Rapids form around rocks, currents move past logs, and streams find pathways of least resistance as rivers flow towards belonging in a greater body of water.

There are often multiple tributaries that join with a river, increasing its flow over time. Even so, that does not make it immune from being depleted. Rivers can run dry before reaching a lake or ocean. Its flow is dependent on receiving more water than it gives to its environment and inhabitants.

Confluences occur when one river joins with another. These have often been considered sacred places in religions. The union of multiple generative forces is something special indeed, expanding and nourishing to both the water and its surroundings. Without rivers, much of our water would be restricted to coastal lands and many forms of life wouldn't exist.

Rivers are sources of life-giving water to those who need it.

Type 2s tend to have a moving and nurturing presence. They desire belonging and bring provision to others as they look to find it. Type 2s can be disruptive if they push too hard with the resources they have to offer or dry up if they get disconnected from the source of their vitality. At the same time, they bring an essential connective energy everywhere they travel. When Type 2s learn to trust the flow of giving and receiving, and find the balance of influencing and conceding, they can find connection and peace. When healthy, Type 2s are a steady flow of sustaining life force.

Reflection Questions for Type 2s:
How am I a resource others as I journey through life with them?
Am I staying connected to the things that fill me up? Am I at risk of becoming depleted?
Where am I finding belonging? Do I experience the peace of my belovedness?

Waves
Enneagram Type 3

Waves do not travel in a line but in a series of peaks and valleys, shifting according to the conditions through which they are moving. While waves travel in a direction, the water itself is actually moving in a circular motion. The dramatic crash onto the shore occurs because of the way the water's orbit has been disrupted. When that crash happens, waves carve coastlines and shift sand.

Oceans are dynamic bodies that are never still and waves are the transmission of energy through its water. That energy transfer can come from the friction between the wind and the water's surface, severe weather, or the movement of the earth. While waves are the outward manifestation of kinetic energy, they are not the source of that energy.

The most powerful waves on the planet are not those that come to the shore, no matter how tall or imposing they may be. It is the waves of the tides that have the greatest impact, causing water to rise and fall at its coastline. This happens due to the force of the moon's gravitational pull bulging the ocean on the side closest to it. In this way, tidal waves form the connection between water and the forces of the universe. They create coastal ecosystems of thriving life, swirling ocean material and organisms through their power.

Waves are a source of fascination and delight. They are sought after by surfers and children, bringing joy through their movement. At the same time, humans find the sound of waves calming, perhaps a reminder of the energy that exists, which they do not have to conjure.

Waves are water in perpetual motion, symbols of vitality and life.

Type 3s tend to have a dynamic presence. They like to stay in motion, working to achieve and move things forward. They do so in a collaborative and communal way, creating habitats for others who come along for the ride. Type 3s can sometimes feel like they are the source of their own energy, forgetting to submit to the deeper work of the universe. When Type 3s learn to trust that their value does not depend on their own hard work, they are able to operate with a deeper authenticity. When healthy, Type 3s bring hope and vitality.

Reflection Questions for Type 3s:
How do I stay in perpetual movement? If I am slowed down, do I crash?
Am I connected to the energy of the universe that flows outside of my own efforts?
Do I experience myself as a valuable and vital part of the world?

Iceberg
Enneagram Type 4

Most of an iceberg exists below the surface. The difference in the densities between freshwater ice and seawater means they float with 90% of their mass below the surface, in the cold and darkness of the deep. When young, icebergs work to establish balance. As that happens, they can flip over entirely, as gravity pulls the heavier side downward.

The substance of icebergs is different from their environment. They float in sea water, but are composed of freshwater, having broken off from glaciers or ice shelves before being set adrift in the sea. Most of the world's icebergs come from the same few sources. In the Northern Hemisphere, most are calved from glaciers in Greenland or Alaska. In the Southern Hemisphere, most are broken from Antartica. As the new iceberg enters the water, it can form large and dangerous waves. Because the sharp edges below the surface pose a danger to ships, icebergs are closely monitored. When an iceberg drifts into shipping routes, it can disrupt the flow of the global economy.

As icebergs move into warmer waters, they melt. As they do so, they make sounds that have sometimes been called singing. Air bubbles that were trapped in the ice pop and sizzle and vibrations hum and roar. When covered in snow icebergs appear white though in actuality, they are a variety of colors, depending on the conditions in which the ice was formed.

Icebergs are water, frozen in such a way that their surroundings are impacted with uniqueness and beauty.

Type 4s tend to have a deep presence. They are not afraid of floating in the cold darkness, which is just as true to their existence as warm light. They can feel alone and disconnected from their surroundings. Sometimes, they can even be seen as disruptive or dangerous. Type 4s can get lost in the struggle for their identity and are helped when they remember the source from which they came. They are not as alone as they feel. When Type 4s learn to trust that everything belongs, both what is above and below, they are able to find the warmth and significance they are looking for. When healthy, Type 4s bring emotional honesty and beauty.

Reflection Questions for Type 4s:
Do I feel adrift and separate from others? What would change if I remembered the source from which I came?
How has my depth been a gift to others? Has it ever been destructive?
Am I experiencing the significance in both what is above and below the surface?

Air & The Head Center Triad
Enneagram Types 5, 6, & 7

Air is the atmosphere of the earth that protects life. It absorbs radiation, creates the pressure needed for water to exist, and retains the heat from the sun. The atmosphere exists in layers, with air pressure and density decreasing further away from the earth's surface. The lowest layer (which is where nearly all water vapor resides) is where most weather events occur. Air holds space for clouds, rain, lightning, wind, and more, all of which provide fundamental nutrients for survival.

It is the circulation of the air that allows heat to be distributed around the earth. Air moves in cells to and from the equator, allowing the heat energy absorbed there to move out towards the poles. When water from lakes and oceans evaporates, it diffuses and becomes part of the air, until it is redistributed through precipitation.

Photons in the air allow humans to see. When light from the sun comes into earth's atmosphere, the photons scatter. Without that process, the light on this planet would carry the intensity of looking directly at the sun.

Air is a key component of the water cycle, which is essential to life on earth.

The Types in the Head Center tend to move above the surface in order to get a better understanding of things. They bring a sense of clarity and guidance as they process their environment through thinking and planning. Head Types work to plan and prepare, which can sometimes feel like a pressure that holds others down. They can struggle with fear as they move in space, wondering how to find support. Head Types are thoughtful and analytical, bringing perspectives that are missed from other vantage points. The processing of Head Types protects and provides for the needs of living things.

- *Priorities*: logic, security, preparation
- *Struggles*: fear and overthinking
- *Strengths*: synthesis, clarity, planning, competency
- *Characteristics*: observing, researching, supporting, conceptualizing

Reflection Questions for Types in the Head Center Triad:
Do I work to maintain a vantage point that sees from above? How have others experienced and responded to my presence?
How have I protected and processed through the kind of space I provide?
When have my contributions felt invisible even though they were essential?

5

Wind
Enneagram Type 5

Wind is the way air moves through space, born from the forces at play in the rotation of the planet. It is formed when increases in pressure, usually from temperature change, cause air to move into lower pressure areas.

Localized pressure changes in smaller regions can also create wind. This happens on sea shores as land and water warm and cool at different rates, and on mountains where the land warms faster than the air. These localized winds carry a force that can change weather patterns and produce dangerous gusts.

Though wind is invisible, it is also powerful and capable. It can push sailboats and carry aircraft. The pattern of trade and westerly winds allowed for the formation of round trip trade routes across the Atlantic and Pacific oceans. The energy of wind can be harnessed by windmills as a renewable and inexhaustible energy source that doesn't pollute the environment. A great deal of human activity and economy is carried by wind.

The strength and impact of wind varies. A light breeze can help creatures cool off on a hot day and a gentle wind can spread seeds to new land in which they can take root. But wind is a potentially dangerous force when it blows strong. It can erode landscapes, spread wildfires, and knock down structures.

Wind ebbs and flows, moving in different directions above the surface, and carrying life from one place to another.

Type 5s tend to have an ethereal presence. They hover above situations to gain an understanding of things. And they see from a different vantage point, allowing for movement that would not be possible without their insights. Type 5s carry a fear that the energy of their movement will run out so they tend to guard themselves and push others away. When Type 5s learn that their ongoing action is enabled by a flow outside themselves, they open up to a deeper connection to their environment. When healthy, Type 5s bring gifts that expand life past old boundaries.

Reflection Questions for Type 5s:
How do I move over and around landscapes as a way of understanding where I am?
Am I connected to the perpetual energy that will continue to flow in and through me? Or am I pushing others away as a means of guarding my energy?
When have I expanded possibilities through the ways I moved and synthesized what was happening?

Clouds
Enneagram Type 6

Clouds are a visible mass of air formed from its saturation with water droplets. This formation happens at a particular temperature known as the dew point. Clouds are made manifest only when conditions are right for their development. They are visual signs of processes at work.

The word cloud comes from the word "clod," meaning a mass of stone or a hill. They were named this because of their similarity in shape to those landforms. Though they are nebulous, like the origin of their name suggests, they are also strong and imposing.

External conditions such as altitude and pressure change how clouds appear. They may exist as low level tufty patches of altocumulus clouds or high level parallel streaks of cirrocumulus clouds. These variations help humans predict weather, as high and wispy cirrus clouds often precede a front, while tall, dense, and dark cumulonimbus clouds show an impending storm. The diversity of cloud formations also sparks the imaginations of children, as generations of them have laid in the grass to talk about the shapes they see.

Earth's ecosystems are changed by the presence of clouds. They help regulate the energy of earth as they absorb infrared energy and reflect solar radiation. Clouds bring relief and shade from the heat of the sun and offer precipitation for the saturation of the earth. Even when clouds bring thunderstorms, it is a provision. Lightning splits atmospheric nitrogen, which reacts with oxygen to create nitrate, a compound plants need to thrive.

Clouds offer prediction, inspiration, protection, and provision to the world around them.

Type 6s tend to have a hardworking presence, experiencing the world through processes. They receive and hold information in ways that help predict outcomes and regulate systems. Type 6s provide for others in ways that are sometimes misunderstood, as they can come off as imposing in their questions. Type 6s process through worst case scenarios and, as such, can struggle with anxiety. The shape they take in response to that anxiety, though, can vary quite a bit from person to person. When Type 6s find the support that comes from the strength of their existence, they express courage and leadership. When healthy, Type 6s inspire humanity towards new futures.

Reflection Questions for Type 6s:
Have I ever been accused of raining on someone's parade? When have my contributions been recognized as a needed provision?
How do I hold the processes that keep life protected and growing?
When has my presence allowed others to predict impending storms before they began?

Rainbow
Enneagram Type 7

Rainbows occur when light is reflected from water droplets in the air. Those water molecules are more dense than the air molecules, which slows down and bends light.

The colors of a rainbow always exist inside sunlight. The water in the air at the place rainbows form reveal those colors through the ways different wavelengths bend differently in response to the water droplets. It is colors brought out from what is already there. The bright colors do not have to be created, conjured or worked for; they only need to be brought out.

When people see rainbows, they tend to respond as if it is a special or even magical experience. They color the sky with brightness, making everything feel a little different because of their presence. The most conspicuous and spectacular rainbows can be seen when there is clear sky in the direction of the sun but shadowy rain clouds still cover the rest. (These are the conditions in which a more rare double rainbow can sometimes appear.) It's the storms and darkness that cause a rainbow to shine more boldly.

It sometimes appears that rainbows move away from people as people move toward them. This happens because the conditions that form a rainbow actually cause many rainbows to exist, but only one can be seen from the vantage point of the viewer. From a different vantage point, it may actually be a different rainbow. They cannot be pinned down.

For generations, rainbows have been symbols of hope.

Type 7s tend to have a bright, colorful presence. They are natural optimists who see life in terms of its possibilities. Type 7s seek adventure and do not like to be restricted, which can make them difficult to pin down. High spirited Type 7s can carry a fear of boredom and pain, as they want to remain lively and energetic. The true vitality of Type 7s is seen most clearly when they make space for pain and light to coexist, no longer avoiding but embracing the tensions of life. When Type 7s slow down and bring out what is hidden, they help others stop to appreciate the marvelousness of each moment. When healthy, Type 7s help others experience life more fully.

Reflection Questions for Type 7s:
How does my presence bring joy and hope to the world? Am I connected to the source of my brightness?
When have I avoided pain? How might darkness hold the key to my brilliance?
Do I experience the magnificence that exists in the present moment?

"We are like prisoners in an unguarded cell. No one confines us against our will, and we have heard that the key that would release us is also locked inside with us. If we could find the key, we could open the door and be free. Yet we do not know where it has been hidden, and even if we knew, part of us is afraid to break out of our prison... With the Enneagram, we have found a master key, one that will unlock many doors."

Don Richard Riso

How We Move & Get Needs Met in the World:
Climate Zones & The Energy Triads

Broadly speaking, there are three distinct climate zones around the earth: tropical, boreal, and temperate. The Tropical Zone exists along the equator, between the Tropic of Cancer and the Tropic of Capricorn and is characterized by its high temperatures and humidity. The Boreal Zone, also known as the Taiga or Polar Zone, is located in a circumpolar belt in the far Northern Hemisphere. It is characterized by long, cold winters and short, cool summers. The Temperate Zone is between the Tropical and the Boreal Zones, and is characterized by moderate temperatures and a wide range of ecosystems.

All three of these climate zones are important and each is distinct in function from one another. In the Enneagram system, the nine Types are divided into three distinct energies* with which we move and get our needs met in the world.

Types 8, 3, and 7 are in the Active Energy Triad. The Types in this Triad ask, "How can I make things happen here?" They take charge when they walk into a room, calling for results and forward progress. Independent and confident, these Types reach out to make change and push past barriers. A time-orientation towards the future means they are planning, moving, and paving the way forward.

Types 9, 4, and 5 are in the Receptive Energy Triad. The Types in this Triad ask, "What is there to process and feel here?" They are reserved when they walk into a room, carrying an open presence and flexible action. Receiving and integrating, these Types provide understanding for themselves and others. A time-orientation towards the past means they are analyzing, ruminating on, or idealizing what has already happened.

Types 1, 2, and 6 are in the Balancing Energy Triad. The Types in this Triad ask, "What is needed or missing here?" They make adjustments when they walk into a room, meeting the expectations they perceive. Responsible and good, these Types advocate for needs and help those around them. A time-orientation towards the present means they are correcting, fulfilling, and troubleshooting what they see.

The Active Energy Triad is like the Tropical Zone, the Receptive Energy Triad is like the Boreal Zone, and the Balancing Energy Triad is like the Temperate Zone. Think about how different the world would be if any one of the Climate Zones were missing. The same is true for humanity. These three different ways of moving and getting our needs met in the world are each valuable. Each Triad offers something important for the flourishing of humanity.

* These Energy Triads are described differently by various Enneagram teachers. Teachers like Riso and Hudson connect to the work of psychoanalyst Karen Horney and use the term "Hornovenian Groups." Other teachers, such as Suzanne Stabile, use "Social Stances." With the language of energies, I am rooting in the work of Dr David Daniels and William M. Schafer, PhD. For more, see the Appendices.

Tropical Zone & The Active Energy Triad
Enneagram Types 8, 3, & 7

The Tropical Zone is characterized by high energy year-round, in the form of both elevated temperatures and strong humidity. This hot and humid weather is essential for the thriving of rainforests. Tropical rainforests produce around 20% of the earth's oxygen and contain over 30 million species of plants and animals— half of the world's wildlife and two-thirds of its plant species. It is an energetic and thriving ecosystem.

    A band of low pressure near the equator is a major driver of global rainfall patterns. The Tropical Zone has only two seasons, not four, and they are based on rainfall, not temperature. These seasons can lead to extreme weather events, including hurricanes, typhoons, heatwaves, and droughts.

    In the midst of this energy, there is also consistency. The closer to the equator, the more predictable and stable the length of days and nights become. At the equator, the sun sets at 6 pm and rises at 6 am every day of the year. The consistently hot, humid, and sunny weather of the Tropical Zone allows crops to grow year-round. It is responsible for producing around 40% of the world's food, from essential crops such as rice and beans to flavorful exports such as bananas, avocados, cocoa, and coffee.

    The Tropical Zone is the productivity center of the planet, providing oxygen, rain, and food for the world.

The Types in the Active Energy Triad are vibrant and productive. They have a high energy that drives them to move with forward action year-round. Their productivity is a needed resource for many. At the same time, Active Types can tend to ignore their feelings and charge ahead when things get difficult, which can be perceived as an imposing heatwave to others. Active Types have a decisive presence oriented towards making things happen, which affects the climate around them. Types in this Triad could benefit from remembering the consistency of sunrise and sunset close to the equator. Every day, there is space for darkness and rest. The Active Triad is independent, energetic, initiating, ambitious, and aspiring.

Reflection Questions for Types in the Active Energy Triad:
How does my active energy and productivity make a positive contribution to the world?
When have I moved too quickly past feelings for the sake of forward motion?
How can I lean into my inner vibrancy with a balance of forward motion and rest?

HOW WE MOVE & GET NEEDS MET IN THE WORLD

8

Mount Merapi
Enneagram Type 8

Merapi means "mountain of fire" in Indonesian, a fitting name for a volcano that has been known to produce ash clouds up to 12 miles high. This mountain of fire is located within the "Ring of Fire," an area of the Pacific known for high levels of seismic activity. Mount Merapi stands over 9,500 feet tall, towering over Java, Indonesia, where it has been continuously erupting for centuries.

The biggest risk Mount Merapi poses is its tendency to produce pyroclastic flows. A pyroclastic flow is a fast-moving mixture of hot gas, ash, and rock fragments that flows down the slopes of a volcano. They can reach speeds of up to 435 miles per hour and temperatures of more than to 1,000 degrees Fahrenheit. Pyroclastic flows can be extremely destructive, as they can engulf everything in their path, including buildings, vegetation, and even people.

Though they can be dangerous, volcanoes like Mount Merapi also have vibrant life around them. They deposit elements like magnesium and potassium when they erupt, producing extremely fertile soils. Once cooled, thin layers of ash can act as natural fertilizer, increasing harvests in years following eruption. In the long term, volcanoes can also create new land, as magma cools into stable new ground that can be inhabited by plants and animals. Furthermore, volcanoes produce natural hot springs. The minerals, heat, and beauty of these unique bodies of water are healing and nurturing for humans and animals alike. As a result, people often choose to both live around and travel to volcanoes.

Humans are drawn to the vibrancy and healing power of Mount Merapi— a place too full of potential to resist.

As a Gut Type in the Active Triad, Type 8s are grounded and strong, like the earth, while also being hot and energetic like the Tropical Zone. Their powerful presence can be like a mountain of fire inside a ring of fire. People may be intimidated by their energy, feeling the way Type 8s can erupt in ways that can overwhelm or engulf others. At the same time, many desire to stay close, drawn to their inner energy and sensing the vitality that surrounds them. The strong energy of a Type 8 can bring life and healing when it is held with awareness and moderation.

Reflection Questions for Type 8s:
When has my forward energy been a force for good?
Are there times when I have erupted in a destructive way?
How might I find more balance in how I hold my power?

3

The Great Barrier Reef
Enneagram Type 3

Coral reefs are underwater ecosystems found in the shallow waters of the tropical oceans around the world. They are formed by coral polyps: small, soft-bodied animals that secrete a hard, calcium carbonate exoskeleton. These exoskeletons form the structure of the reef, and over time, they can create large and complex systems.

The Great Barrier Reef is the largest coral reef system in the world, stretching over 1,400 miles and covering an area of about 133,000 square miles. The growing exoskeletons of its corals provide habitat, shelter, and food for marine life. The Reef is home to more than 1,500 species of fish, 400 species of coral, and an estimated 30% of the world's species of marine plants.

Though the exoskeleton of corals makes them appear strong, they are actually quite sensitive. When corals experience stress, they expel the colorful algae that live in their tissues, leaving their white skeleton exposed. This event, known as "bleaching," puts coral at greater risk of starvation and disease. In the last decade, rising ocean temperatures have caused widespread bleaching in the Great Barrier Reef, putting the entire ecosystem at risk. Efforts are being made to protect the site for future generations. UNESCO recognizes this reef as a World Heritage Site because of its extraordinary value to the global ecosystem.

The Great Barrier Reef is a natural wonder, teeming with life, overflowing with beauty, and carrying ecological importance for the world.

As a Heart Type in the Active Triad, Type 3s are nourishing and connective, like water, while also being hot and energetic like the Tropical Zone. Their dynamic presence can grow ecosystems that create shelter for others. At the same time, when they aren't connected to their own sensitivity, they can leave those ecosystems vulnerable. They can expel the very thing that keeps them safe and growing. People are drawn to the dynamic beauty of Type 3s in action, desiring to witness and be part of what they create. The connective energy of a Type 3 can bring growth and value when held with honesty and vulnerability.

Reflection Questions for Type 3s:
When has my dynamic energy created ecosystems?
Am I more sensitive than I let myself see? To what?
How might I be more honest about both my value and my vulnerability?

7

Hurricane
Enneagram Type 7

Hurricanes are formed over the warm ocean waters of the tropics. These warm ocean waters become fuel for the engine of an emerging tropical storm, which decreases in energy only once it encounters land. Competing pressures and forces create a rotation of strong winds around an "eye" at a hurricane's center. An "eyewall" of dense clouds and high pressure keep this center of the storm seemingly unaffected by its own force.

Their energy is impossible to ignore, as their size reaches up to 10 miles high and 1,000 miles across. When they reach land, hurricanes often cause significant destruction, with flooding from their rain and storm surges, as well as uprooted trees and destroyed buildings from their winds.

Though they can be destructive, hurricanes also provide needed climate effects. Their size makes them strong enough to move equatorial heat to reach wider zones of the earth. After making landfall, hurricanes spread rainfall to wide inland zones, providing important nourishment for vegetation. Hurricane winds also benefit the inland zones, as they can carry spores and seeds, increasing their spread and potential for life. Coral reefs in particular benefit from the way hurricanes pull their energy from the ocean, lowering its temperature and reducing thermal stress for the coral. The strong waves caused by hurricanes can also carry away invasive algae from the reef.

Without hurricanes, heat, rain, and energy would get stuck at the equator, instead of reaching out to the breadths of the earth.

As a Head Type in the Active Triad, Type 7s are clarifying and synthesizing, like air, while also being hot and energetic like the Tropical Zone. Type 7s have an inner engine fueled by excitement in their surrounding environment. Their seemingly boundless energy can be a power that sweeps up those around them, and Type 7s can struggle to see that destructive wake. This chaotic spin becomes less volatile when Type 7s connect with grounding practices and a calm center. With awareness, the expansive energy of a Type 7 can change the climate around them and carry ideas further and faster than others, becoming a true force for good.

Reflection Questions for Type 7s:
When has my expansive energy changed climates and spread potential?
Am I causing more disruption than I let myself feel? How are others affected by me?
What grounding practices can help me quiet the winds of how I show up?

Boreal Zone & The Receptive Energy Triad
Enneagram Types 9, 4, & 5

The Boreal Zone is characterized by long, cold winters and short, cool summers. It is found in the high latitudes of the Northern Hemisphere. A large portion of this zone is an enormous space of woodland that, from outer space, looks like a green band encircling the top of the globe. This boreal woodland makes up almost one third of the world's forests, and is the largest zone of the earth relatively undisturbed by human development.

Coniferous trees make up most of the boreal forest, as they are equipped to survive the specifics of this climate. Their narrow needles have waxy coatings which protect the trees from drying winds, and remain green year round, allowing conifers to photosynthesize on warmer days in the winter. The boreal zone includes not only forests, but wetlands and tundra.

The shifting light of the Boreal Zone is one of its most unique features. Some parts have what is known as the "midnight sun," days and weeks in which there is never a sunset. In Svalbard, Norway, the northernmost inhabited region of Europe, there is no sunset from April 19 to August 23. This is countered by the "polar night," in which the brightest it gets in the winter is a faint glow of light at midday. In Svalbard, this lasts from November 11 to January 30.

The Boreal Zone stores large amounts of carbon in its trees, soils, and peat; controlling temperatures and mitigating climate change for the entire earth.

The Types in the Receptive Energy Triad are retreating and integrating. They store what they see and experience, allowing the energy to simmer until they feel ready to bring it forward. They need space to escape from the chaos of human development, cultivating their natural imaginativeness. This withdrawal can feel aloof, dark, or cold to others when it excludes action or gets stuck in the past. The Types in this Triad may need to be reminded of their capacity to operate in long periods of bright creativity when resourced and aware. The Receptive Triad can be described as perceptive, contemplative, reflective, listening, and distinct.

Reflection Questions for Types in the Receptive Energy Triad:
How does my receptive energy bring integration and imagination to those around me?
When have I been overwhelmed by storing too much or waiting too long to take action?
How can I lean into my creativity with a balance of forward action and inner retreat?

9

Norwegian Fjords
Enneagram Type 9

Norwegian fjords are long and narrow inlets of the sea that are bordered by steep cliffs, sometimes more than 4,000 feet from top to bottom. They were formed by glaciers that went below sea level. When those glaciers retreated, they carved deep u-shaped valleys whose floors were flooded by the sea waters.

Norway is not the only place to have fjords, as they exist in other glacially affected countries around the world. What is unique is the quantity in Norway and the way the fjords affect the coastline. Norway has nearly 1,200 fjords that give it 18,000 miles of coast. However, if you exclude the fjords, Norway would have only 1,600 miles of coast. Fjords maximize and expand the connecting points between land and sea.

Fjord is from the word *fjoror* which means "where you travel across." They are deep enough to allow boats, especially ferries and even cruise ships, to pass through and over them. Fjords are also crossed by car and train, through both bridges and underwater tunnels. The deep water of Norwegian fjords are teeming with life, and known to be prolific places for fishing. This may be, in part, because of the recent discovery of coral reefs living deep at their base, playing host to thousands of species of marine life. There are Viking towns and fishing villages that have been in the fjords for more than 1,000 years.

The Norwegian fjords are places of crossing, life, and beauty visited by thousands year after year.

As a Gut Type in the Receptive Triad, Type 9s are grounded and strong, like the earth, while also retreating and integrating like the Boreal Zone. Their past carved them into people whose energy provides a spaciousness for the energy of others. Type 9s can hold life, build bridges, expand networks, and release potential. At the same time, Type 9s can lose track of themselves while doing so, not recognizing their own beauty and fortitude. The spacious energy of a Type 9 can maximize connection when held in balance with power.

Reflection Questions for Type 9s:
When has my receptive energy made space for connection and life?
Are there times I have lost track of myself while building bridges for others?
How might I find more balance in how I retreat and stand strong?

4

Lake Baikal
Enneagram Type 4

Lake Baikal is the largest freshwater lake by volume in the world, containing approximately 20% of the world's unfrozen surface fresh water. It is more than 400 miles long and in some places, over one mile deep. It is located in Siberia, Russia and despite its massive size, completely freezes over in the winter.

Over 2,500 species of plants and animals call Lake Baikal home, including many endemic to the lake and found nowhere else on the planet. One of the most famous of these creatures is the nerpa, the only species of freshwater seal in the world. Lake Baikal is known for its clear, blue water. It is possible to see more than 100 feet down during spring and in the winter, walk on transparent ice. Many indigenous communities revere Lake Baikal as a sacred place and source of spiritual healing and renewal, sometimes referring to it as the "Sacred Sea."

The largest rift zone on the planet runs beneath Lake Baikal. This crack in the Earth's crust means the lake itself does not have a solid bottom but a collection of sediments that have been filling the lower part of the crack for millions of years. These sediments are like bogs which release methane gas, forming patterns of bubbles that get frozen into the lake in winter. Historically, the fact that this was an isolated lake allowed its unique culture and biology to thrive. However, as people have grown aware of its uniqueness and beauty, tourism has increased from just a few thousand people a few decades ago to three million people per year today.

Lake Baikal is considered one of the most important freshwater ecosystems in the world.

As a Heart Type in the Receptive Triad, Type 4s are nourishing and connective like water, while also retreating and integrating like the Boreal Zone. Type 4s desire deep authenticity no matter the season, and can be vessels through which others see life more clearly. Though some Type 4s seem calm on the surface, all have a deep crack of inner turmoil that raises questions of whether something is missing in them. They can get lost and overwhelmed in those depths if they aren't careful. However, if Type 4s learn to fill that crack with groundedness, they can rise up into creativity and engagement. The deep energy of a Type 4 can help themselves and others recognize that each are in fact unique.

Reflection Questions for Type 4s:
When has my receptive energy helped others see more authentically?
Are there times I have gotten lost in my inner questioning?
How might I find balance in how I dive deep in retreat and rise up to engagement?

5

Aurora Borealis
Enneagram Type 5

The Aurora Borealis are named after Aurora, the Roman goddess of dawn, Boreas, the Greek name for the north wind. In other words, they are "the wind of the dawn." Otherwise known as the Northern Lights, they are colorful glowing beams that appear close while actually moving about 80 miles above the ground. These lights occur after electrically charged particles from solar storms make it to the earth and crash into the atmosphere. The particles are captured in the magnetic field, heat up the gas of our atmosphere, and accelerate towards the poles. This means the normally invisible magnetic field of the earth becomes lit up with color.

Different gasses give off different hues when heated, so the Aurora Borealis is most commonly seen in shades of green (the reaction of oxygen). But it can also appear blue, pink, or purple, the reaction of nitrogen. The intensity of colors and light varies, with some displays faint and scattered, and others bright and vivid. The Aurora is most visible during the winter, when nights are longer and the sky is clearer.

Many cultures around the world have legends about the Northern Lights. The Vikings believed they were reflections of the Valkyries' armor leading warriors to Odin. In Finland, the lights were called "fire fox," as they pictured foxes running through the sky, lighting it with sparks as their tails brushed the mountains. In Greenland, they believed the lights were the spirits of children who had died, dancing across the sky.

Most people who have seen the Aurora Borealis recognize it as a once-in-a-lifetime experience that they hold as a precious memory.

As a Head Type in the Receptive Triad, Type 5s are clarifying and synthesizing, like air, while also retreating and integrating like the Boreal Zone. Type 5s appear to be closer than they are, as they keep the world at a distance and prefer the space of observation. This position offers a unique vantage point that can make what was previously unseen visible and fascinating. They are tempted to hoard energy for later use, in order to maintain the capacity to learn and retreat. But if they allow themselves instead to react, they light things up with a special grandeur. With a balance of distance and engagement, the perspective energy of Type 5s shows us new possibilities.

Reflection Questions for Type 5s:
When has my receptive energy shown things people wouldn't have otherwise noticed?
Am I too far from the world, stuck in the energy of observation and retreat?
How can I allow myself to engage with possibilities and show new perspectives?

HOW WE MOVE & GET NEEDS MET IN THE WORLD

Temperate Zone & The Balancing Energy Triad
Enneagram Types 1, 2, & 6

The Temperate Zone is found in the middle latitudes of the earth between the Tropical and Boreal Zones. Every continent except Antarctica has at least a small portion of land in the Temperate Zone. It has four distinct seasons: spring, summer, autumn, and winter. Though characterized by more moderate temperatures overall, this zone has a greater temperature range, from below zero degrees Farenheit in the winter to 90 degrees or more in the summer.

External conditions such as ocean currents, topography, and wind have a large effect on the climate of the Temperate Zone. Ocean currents carry warm or cold water from one area to another and cause the coastal zones to be warmer or cooler than they would be otherwise. Mountains disrupt the flow of wind and rain to create microclimates where one side is wet and rainy and the other is dry, or where high elevations are cold and the base is warm. Westerly winds bring warm moist air from the ocean to land, carrying with them more moderate temperatures and higher precipitation.

A variety of landscapes, including deciduous forests, grasslands, and savannas, are found in the Temperate Zone. Though the Temperate Zone is more stable than the Tropical and Boreal Zones, it is also prone to extremes like heatwaves, blizzards, tornadoes, and thunderstorms.

The Temperate Zone has the greatest agricultural production and the most world population centers of all Climate Zones of the earth.

The Types in the Balancing Energy Triad are moderate and adjusting. They react to external conditions, and shift according to perceived expectations. They aim to be responsible and good advocates, able to change according to what is needed in different seasons. Though they perceive themselves as balanced and temperate, they can carry extremes when stress pushes them into rigidity and a sense of superiority. The Types in this Triad need to learn to make choices that care for the life within them independent of internal or external expectations. The Balancing Triad can be described as responsible, dedicated, sacrificial, committed, hardworking, and diligent.

Reflection Questions for Types in the Balancing Energy Triad:
How does my balancing energy in social settings promote the greater good?
When have I become rigid, and sought to control instead of harmonize?
How can I expand from the effort to meet expectations into the flexibility of giving and receiving care?

1

North American Prairie
Enneagram Type 1

The North American Prairie is a vast grassland ecosystem stretching from Canada to Mexico. Its ecosystem has creative ways of working with environmental pressures to sustain itself. The long roots of prairie grasses reach deep underground, enabling them to withstand winds and prevent erosion. The migratory nature of the bison and other grazing herds that call it home allow for cycles of regeneration. Fire stops trees and other species from invading the prairie, while also burning dead vegetation and clearing space for new growth. Meanwhile, the deep roots of the perennial flowers allow them to grow back quickly when the fire burns out.

Prairie soils tend to be deep and fertile, allowing for high crop productivity. This is why it became an important agricultural region for worldwide food production of wheat, corn, soybeans, and more. It is also why it has become one of the world's most threatened ecosystems, with only 1% of tallgrass and about 25% of mid and shortgrass prairie lands remaining. During the Great Depression, overfarming in this region meant there were not enough deep-rooted grasses to hold the soil in place during significant drought and high winds, giving parts of this region the nickname of the Dust Bowl.

The high winds of the prairie are now being leveraged as an opportunity. In the U.S., wind turbines are 8% of the energy profile, and have the capacity to electrify 20 million average homes. Almost the entire North American Prairie holds the required average wind speeds to support wind turbines, giving it a new nickname, the Saudi Arabia of Wind.

The North American Prairie is and has been depended upon as a source of sustenance, and now energy, for humans around the globe.

As a Gut Type in the Balancing Triad, Type 1s are grounded and strong, like the earth, while also being moderate and adjusting, like the Temperate Zone. They are suited for resilience in the face of stressors, working with responsibility to hold environments together, and committing to regrow after facing fire. They are driven and thorough, sometimes losing their rootedness for the sake of productivity. As they work to improve, Type 1s respond to people and situations by noticing what could be better. This critiquing energy of a Type 1 can feel like winds of destruction, but can also be a source of power when harnessed with thoughtfulness.

Reflection Questions for Type 1s:
When has my balancing energy improved situations or held things together?
Are there times I have lost my rootedness by working too hard towards a goal?
How can I balance my critiques with thoughtfulness, for myself and others?

2

Merced National Wildlife Refuge
Enneagram Type 2

The Merced National Wildlife Refuge in central California, east of San Francisco, covers more than 10,200 acres and is part of the National Wildlife Refuge System. It was established in 1951 to serve as a sanctuary for migratory waterfowl. It is named after its nearest town, as well as the Merced River, which runs through it.

Thousands of birds stop at Merced during their annual migrations. In fact, about 20,000 sandhill cranes and 60,000 snow geese end their flights from the north and winter at Merced. It is also a breeding ground for hawks, blackbirds, marsh wrens, mallards, and burrowing owls. The more than 200 species of birds that live in or visit Merced Refuge make it a popular destination for birdwatchers and wildlife researchers.

In addition to the river and wetlands as a water source, Merced Refuge has unique vernal pools that form in the winter. Vernal pools form when natural shallow craters fill with rainwater. As the pools take shape, tadpole shrimp emerge from cysts that were nested in the dirt the previous year. These shrimp, along with other aquatic invertebrates who make the pools home, provide food for the migrating and wintering birds. When the vernal pools evaporate in spring, they fill with wildflowers. John Muir called this sight the "floweriest part of the world." In addition to these rivers, wetlands, and pools, Merced Refuge also cultivates more than 300 acres of corn and winter wheat, and manages irrigated pastures and native grasslands. These fields are important sources of food for cranes who shelter there.

Merced means mercy in Spanish, an appropriate name for such a sanctuary for life.

As a Heart Type in the Balancing Triad, Type 2s are nourishing and connective like water, while also being moderate and adjusting, like the Temperate Zone. Type 2s examine what is needed in the environment around them and seek to provide that missing link. They can offer different things in different seasons, making them a refuge for many. At the same time, Type 2s can forget that they do not have the capacity or ability to provide everything for those they care about, and can benefit from allowing space for separation without fear of losing importance. When they admit their generosity has limits, and allow the pools they offer to run dry, Type 2s experience the surprising beauty that emerges from the newly created space.

Reflection Questions for Type 2s:
When has my balancing energy provided for the needs of others?
Are there times I have not given people the space they needed?
What new possibilities might emerge if I allow my generosity to run dry?

6

Autumn
Enneagram Type 6

In the Temperate Zone, the seasons are caused by the Earth's tilt on its axis. The length of the seasons varies by location within the temperate zone, with the seasons generally lasting longer in higher latitudes and shorter in lower latitudes. Though both winter and summer exist in the Boreal Zone to a certain extent, and summer exists in the Tropical Zone, autumn as an extended and distinct season is unique to the Temperate Zone.

Autumn is marked by both a decrease in temperatures and in daylight hours. It typically occurs between the months of September and November in the Northern Hemisphere and between March and June in the Southern Hemisphere. It is a time of planning and work, as kids return to school and crops become ready to harvest. For many years of human history, autumn was the time to focus on preparing for winter. It is also a time of beauty as the leaves of deciduous trees change color, turning shades of red, yellow, and orange before falling off the tree. As the sunlight decreases, the chlorophyll breaks down and reveals the true colors that have been hidden below.

The autumnal equinox is one of only two times in the Temperate Zone when the daylight and evening hours are equal. It occurs between September 20th and 24th in the Northern Hemisphere and marks the transition from summer to fall. The full moon that occurs closest to the autumnal equinox carries the special name of *Harvest Moon*. The moonrise of the Harvest Moon comes soon after sunset, and shines brilliantly early in the evening. Traditionally, this extra light enabled farmers to work later to harvest their crops and gave this seasonal moonrise its distinct name.

Autumn is a colorful season of beauty, transition, and productivity that helps humans move with the rhythms of the seasons.

As a Head Type in the Balancing Triad, Type 6s are clarifying and synthesizing, like air, while also being moderate and adjusting, like the Temperate Zone. Type 6s are focused on planning and working, wanting everything to be lined up for the future. The way they operate can fade outer exteriors and reveal the true colors of those around them. Though Type 6s like predictability and rules, they need to remember that evenness is rare and short-lived. The preparing energy of Type 6 can bring a needed productivity to their environments.

Reflection Questions for Type 6s:
When has my balancing energy helped others be prepared or appreciate depth?
Am I trying too hard to make things equal or fair that may need to instead be accepted?
How can I allow myself to be open to each new season as it comes?

"Once personality is formed, attention becomes immersed in the preoccupations that characterize our type. We lose the essential, childlike ability to respond to the world as it really is and begin to become selectively sensitive to the information that supports our type's world view. We see what we need to see in order to survive and become oblivious to the rest."

Helen Palmer

How We React to & Cope with the World:
Animal Groupings & The Harmonic Triads

All animals need access to water, shelter, and food. There are three distinct groups of animals, based upon the different foods they eat: carnivores, herbivores, and omnivores. Animals that eat mostly meat are considered carnivores, animals that eat only plants are considered herbivores, and animals that eat both are considered omnivores. Teeth can often be a sign of what group an animal belongs to, as herbivores typically have flat teeth designed to chew up vegetation, carnivores have sharp teeth designed to rip into meat, and omnivores have some combination of the two. Animals in each grouping can be big or small, and live in a variety of habitats. What they have in common is what and how they consume.

All three of these animal groupings are important for the functioning of the earth's ecosystems and all carry distinct features from one another. In the Enneagram system, the nine Types are divided into three separate conflict styles or harmonic patterns* with which they react to and cope with the world.

Types 8, 4, and 6 are in the Reactivity Triad. The Types in this Triad cope by feeling intensity and emotion, with a tendency to become emotionally reactive during conflict or stress. They have intense feelings and thoughts, which they hope will be mirrored by those around them. In conflict or difficult situations, they focus on self-reliance and injustice as they take the lead (Type 8s), want to be seen, understood, and supported (Type 4s), or feel anxious as they look for both support and independence (Type 6s).

Types 9, 2, and 7 are in the Positivity Triad. The Types in this Triad cope by reframing or avoiding adversity, with a tendency to put an optimistic spin on conflict or stress. They reframe negative thoughts and feelings, which they hope will bring more contentment to themselves and others. In conflict or difficult situations, they avoid or deny what is happening in order to avoid disruption (Type 9s), focus on the needs of others (Type 2s), or seek exciting and positive alternatives (Type 7s).

Types 1, 3, and 5 are in the Competency Triad. The Types in this Triad cope by using analysis and problem solving, with a tendency to stay rational during conflict or stress. They emotionally detach and stay calm, which they hope will bring objectivity and resolution to the problem. In conflict or difficult situations, they use logic to assess what went wrong in order to fix and improve it (Type 1s), create a plan for repair in order to feel achievement (Type 3s), or learn about the context in order to be confident about a solution (Type 5s).

The Reactivity Triad is like carnivores, the Positivity Triad is like herbivores, and the Competency Triad is like omnivores. Think about how different the world would be if any one of these animal groupings were missing. The same is true for humanity. These three different ways of reacting to and coping with the world are each valuable. Each Triad offers something important for the flourishing of humanity.

Dr. David Daniels calls these the Emotional Regulation Triads, with the labels of Sustaining-Expressing (Types 8, 4, and 6), Reframing-Shifting (Types 9, 2, and 7), and Containing-Rationale (Types 1, 3, and 5).

Carnivores & The Reactivity Triad
Enneagram Types 8, 4, & 6

As the top tier of the food chain, carnivores keep the populations of other animals in check. Naturalists have found that the reintroduction of carnivores positively affects entire ecosystems through the ways they control overpopulation. In Yellowstone National Park, the reintroduction of wolves had such a dramatic influence that the path of a river changed and a number of species returned.

The adaptations of carnivores are designed to make them more responsive hunters. They are often strong or fast, and are equipped with exceptionally sharp senses of sight, sound, and smell. For them, a single missed meal can spell the difference between survival and death. Their digestive systems are designed with a high stomach-volume to intestine-volume ratio that allows them to eat a large amount of food at once, and be sustained by that for a week or longer.

Compared to herbivorous mammals like deer and horses, carnivores are some of the loudest animals on Earth. Their calls are means of asserting dominance, initiating courtship, or warning others of danger. Carnivores can also communicate nonverbally: via scent or via body language. Historically, large carnivores have vast territories of dozens or even hundreds of miles as they move around to hunt for food. Many are solitary and territorial inside of this home-range.

The intensity of carnivores impacts their surrounding environment in significant ways.

The Types in the Reactivity Triad are generally passionate in the face of difficulty, with a focus on the depth or complexity of a problem. They tend to work themselves up when something happens and have a hard time containing their emotions and opinions. They cope by feeling the problem before moving on to deal with the issue that caused it. Reactivity Types tend to be loud about displaying and communicating their concerns and frustrations. Their untamed reaction is a way to hunt for the truth of where the people around them stand. They struggle to hold the balance between independence and interdependence, and can become territorial or defensive when trust is broken or not yet built.

Reflection Questions for Types in the Reactivity Triad:
How has my reactivity helped to reveal the underlying feelings and issues that needed to be addressed in a time of conflict?
When have I intimidated others with my intensity, emotion, or communication?
How can I open myself to more trust and less defensiveness in how I react to others?

8

Cheetah
Enneagram Type 8

Cheetahs are the fastest land animals on the planet. They are capable of going from 0 to 60 mph in just 3 seconds and at full speed, they cover about 21 feet with each stride. The pads of most cats' paws are soft, but the cheetahs' pads are hard like the rubber on a tire. Yet, it is not the speed of cheetahs that provides their greatest attribute for hunting but their agility. Their claws provide extra grip when sprinting, and their tails can act as rudders. This combination allows cheetahs to jump sideways, change directions quickly, and slow down almost instantly.

The sharp eyesight of cheetahs allows them to pick out prey from a distance. The black marks below their eyes help absorb the glare of the sun. When cheetahs spot prey, they run hard so they can avoid competition by pouncing and eating quickly. Additionally, cheetahs only need to drink water every three or four days, a stamina enabling them to roam great distances in search of food. Cheetahs can't roar, but they do purr when content and growl when facing danger.

A female raises her cubs alone, hiding them in dens by day and teaching them her hunting skills as they grow. The cubs have a smoky colored, long, wooly coat that acts as camouflage, concealing the cubs while their mothers seek places to den that will protect them from predators. The vulnerability of cubs means many do not survive the first year, but if they do, after that first year, they can hunt on their own.

Cheetahs are agile, sharp, and protective animals who move with endurance and focus.

As a Gut Type in the Reactivity Triad, Type 8s are grounded and strong, like the earth, while also being intense and territorial like carnivores. Type 8s want their feelings and opinions known when they are facing difficulties. They often respond hard and fast, taking the lead, controlling the direction, and pushing others to see the injustice in the situation. Type 8s have a desire to protect vulnerability in themselves and others and are quick to confront and challenge something that threatens. Their coping strategy is to react to conflict or pain with intensity in order to stay in touch with their own strength and agility to conquer it. When healthy, the speed and agility with which Type 8s move toward conflicts helps bring honest conversation and forward momentum.

Reflection Questions for Type 8s:
When has my reactivity and intensity protected others and pushed for justice?
Are there times when others have been intimidated by my confrontations?
How might I get more comfortable displaying my vulnerability alongside my strength?

4

Octopus
Enneagram Type 4

Octopuses are solitary creatures who live alone in dens. When needed, they use their powerful arms to move rocks to create a door they can pull closed from the inside. They are masters of camouflage, matching the colors and even textures of their surroundings so they can hide in plain sight. If a predator gets too close, octopuses can dart away quickly by shooting water from a muscular tube called a siphon. If this doesn't work, they can release a cloud of black ink, which both obscures the vision and dulls the sense of the creature that gets too close.

There is a consensus in the field of animal science that octopuses are conscious beings. Their arms are not only strong but intelligent, holding two-thirds of an octopus' neurons. Its suckers taste, touch, and feel with refined detail. Octopuses are smart enough to avoid places where they previously experienced negative stimuli, even when free of struggle in that moment. They both feel pain and remember pain.

When researcher Sy Montgomery visited a sick octopus named Octavia, whom she had previously spent time with, Octavia emerged from the depths of the tank where she had been hiding for 10 months. She accepted a fish offered by Montgomery but set it aside. It was a desire for connection, not hunger, that brought this octopus to the surface. Before returning to her den, Octavia extended her suckers to Montgomery, looked her in the face, and held onto her arm.

Octopuses are intelligent creatures, who hold memories of feelings and exhibit a capacity for emotional connection.

As a Heart Type in the Reactivity Triad, Type 4s are nourishing and connective like water, while also being intense and territorial like carnivores. Type 4s have a desire to actualize their true identity and will taste, touch, and feel with great detail to process the depth of what's around them. They want to find someone who understands those feelings, while simultaneously tending to camouflage or withdraw in order to avoid abandonment. Their coping strategy is to internalize the experience of conflict or pain in order to feel the fullness of the emotion. When healthy, the depth with which Type 4s remember and engage with the pain of conflict helps cultivate emotional authenticity and greater intimacy.

Reflection Questions for Type 4s:
When has my reactivity and emotionality brought connection and depth?
Are there times when I felt abandoned because I withdrew, not because another left?
How could I balance my internalized experiences with connection and compromise?

6

Burrowing Owl
Enneagram Type 6

Burrowing owls are active during the day. Their small size and camouflage coloring allow them to blend into their environment while searching for insects and small mammals on the ground. The diet of burrowing owls is adaptable to whatever food is available, including grasshoppers, beetles, lizards, mice, and more, saving extras for slow hunting days. Before laying eggs, these creative planners scatter animal dung near the entrance of their burrows to attract troops of dung beetles, which allows the owls to find food without leaving home.

The nests of burrowing owls are usually in abandoned holes dug by other animals, such as prairie dogs. These burrows regulate temperatures and keep the owls from becoming dehydrated during hot weather. When burrowing owls are threatened by predators, they make calls that mimic the sound of rattlesnakes. This works especially well when they are hidden in their burrows since the predator can't know if there's a rattlesnake underground.

Mating pairs of burrowing owls are loyal to one another and take care of each other. Males may deliver food to the females, and both members groom and preen each other as well as rub beaks together. Parents take turns incubating the eggs for the 4 weeks it takes them to hatch. These pairs nest in loose colonies of up to 100 individuals or more, who warn each other of danger and take turns standing guard near the nest burrows.

Burrowing owls are clever, observant, and resourceful animals, who are creative in the ways they support one another.

As a Head Type in the Reactivity Triad, Type 6s are clarifying and synthesizing, like air, while also being intense and territorial like carnivores. Type 6s react defensively against negative situations by either hiding in plain sight with their guard up or burrowing underground, seeking someone else to stand guard. They focus on assessing situations, planning for future needs, and looking for support. They are committed and reliable members of their community but can struggle to trust others. Their coping strategy is to watch for danger, threats, and conflicts, in order to react before anything bad happens. When healthy, the interdependence and preparedness valued by Type 6s promote the greater good of all.

Reflection Questions for Type 6s:
When has my reactivity and preparedness brought safety and communal care?
Are there times when my vigilance and guardedness have created barriers?
How could I balance my future planning with an openness to the present moment?

Herbivores & The Positivity Triad
Enneagram Types 9, 2, & 7

Herbivores are plant-eaters who feed on fruit, leaves, wood, nectar, or seeds. Because they feed on plants, which are primary producers, herbivores are known as primary consumers. Primary consumers form the link between the photosynthesized energy produced by plants and the greater ecosystem and food chain around them.

Animals ranging in size from beetles to elephants are herbivores. No matter their size, they are selective in what they consume, choosing high quality and nutritious plants first in order to meet their daily energy needs. In addition, some herbivores are known to feed on a variety of plants so they can both balance their diet and avoid consuming too much of any one type of defensive chemical.

The teeth and digestive tracts of herbivores are designed to aid in the work of breaking down fibrous material. Many have several stomach chambers and are called ruminants. Ruminants regurgitate and rechew food to help with the processing. Furthermore, there is a cycle of co-evolution of plant defense and herbivore offense, with the digestive systems of herbivores finding ways to get around the negative defenses plants throw at them.

Herbivores are selective and evolved eaters, able to process, counteract, or avoid the toxins plants produce in order to find the nutrients they need.

The Types in the Positivity Triad are generally optimistic in the face of difficulty, with a focus on reframing or avoiding problems. They are selective in what they consume— choosing what makes them and others feel good and avoiding what doesn't. Positivity Types want contentment for themselves and others, which means they would tend towards keeping everyone happy instead of dealing with difficulty. This Triad tries to put a positive spin on difficult feelings or conflict, looking for ways to make negative situations easier to digest. As a result, they tend to reframe disappointments in a positive light instead of taking the needed time to ruminate in the pain.

Reflection Questions for Types in the Positivity Triad:
How has my positivity helped bring optimism and hope to difficult situations?
When have I avoided negative feelings or situations that should have been addressed?
How can I open to more non-binary patterns, in which pain and goodness can co-exist?

Elephant
Enneagram Type 9

Elephants are social. They form bond groups, traveling and living with one or two families besides their own. During the dry season, these bond groups cluster together and form female-led clans that protect and defend one another. Though male elephants are typically more solitary, they too are social when not competing for dominance or mates.

The size of elephants, along with their resilient skulls and thick skin, makes them nearly invulnerable to carnivorous predators. Not only that, their trunks and tusks provide adaptability and strength, allowing them to touch, grasp, dig, and defend. Their trunks also allow them to sound the alarm to protect others in their clan. They stroke or wrap their trunks together as a way of greeting. Elephants are also known to communicate by producing and sensing seismic vibrations in the earth.

Both Asian and African elephants migrate, living in diverse habitats, traveling during the dry season to find food, and having a huge impact on any environment they enter. When they uproot trees, which is one of their habits, elephants transform forests into grasslands. During droughts, when they dig for water, the holes they create are able to be used by other animals as well. As they bathe, elephants enlarge existing water holes with their movements. Perhaps this environmental impact is why the expression "there's an elephant in the room" came to refer to something obvious that is being ignored or unaddressed.

Elephants are caring, migratory, and tough creatures who impact their environments in significant ways.

As a Gut Type in the Positivity Triad, Type 9s are grounded and strong, like the earth, while also being migratory and contentment-focused like herbivores. Type 9s form strong bonds with the people around them and don't want to see bad or difficult things in themselves or anyone else. So, when difficulty becomes difficult to digest, they move on to find comfort elsewhere. They often communicate non-verbally, through touch and vibrations more than words. Type 9s can become overwhelmed by needs, as they struggle with their simultaneous desires for autonomy and merging. Though Type 9s are peaceful, they are also tough and stubborn. Their coping strategy is to carry the weight of things in order to maintain stability. When healthy, Type 9s bring an strong yet peaceful presence that helps create harmony.

Reflection Questions for Type 9s:
When has my positivity and calm brought harmony in times of conflict?
Are there times when I have avoided or ignored things that needed to be dealt with?
How might I get more comfortable with displaying my strength and autonomy?

2

Beaver
Enneagram Type 2

Beavers focus their energy on building homes. They use trees and shrubs as building material for dams, which stops flowing water and creates ponds teeming with life. Water gives them a refuge from land predators, allows them to move building objects more easily, and provides them a space to swim and play. The eyes, ears and nostrils of beavers are arranged so that they can remain above water when the rest of the body submerges.

    The core of beaver social organization is a family composed of a monogamous pair and their offspring. They form bonds through mutual grooming and play fighting, rarely being aggressive with one another. The family expects its young to help as soon as they are able, repairing dams and lodges and assisting with raising any new offspring. Their lodges, which offer protection from both predators and difficult weather conditions, are often shared with other animals like muskrats and otters.

    The landscape and biodiversity of an area is greatly affected by the presence of beavers. They are ecosystem engineers, whose dams alter the paths of streams and establish new wetland habitats. Those wetlands then help remove sediments and pollutants from rivers and stop the loss of important soils. The presence of beavers increases wild salmon and trout populations, which use the newly created ponds for spawning, overwintering, and feeding. These fish, in turn, increase the presence of fish-eating birds in the area.

    Beavers are industrious home builders, who create communities and provide resources for those around them.

As a Heart Type in the Positivity Triad, Type 2s are nourishing and connective like water, while also being migratory and contentment-focused like herbivores. Type 2s are builders of support systems, who tend to ignore the difficulties in their own life in order to work hard for others. They focus on their image of being caring and self-sacrificing, hoping they will be loved because of the ways they have provided for others. Type 2s often learned to jump in and help when they were young, as a way of supporting their family and friend groups. Their coping strategy is to focus on their positive qualities, while repressing negative thoughts or feelings. When healthy, Type 2s change the environment of conflict to be a place where each person, including themselves, feels supported.

Reflection Questions for Type 2s:

When has my positivity and support helped others feel seen in times of conflict?
Are there times when I have repressed my own motivation, needs, or feelings?
How can I build environments of mutuality in which I both give and receive?

7

Goldfinch
Enneagram Type 7

Goldfinches get their name because of their bright color. Even in the midst of the differences between males and females and the periodic variations in brightness, every type, in every season, is always a shade of yellow.

Their preferred habitat is open country. They love to have the space of fields, meadows, roadsides, and orchards. They wait to build their nests and breed until mid-to-late summer when thistle seeds and down are easy to find. Before that point, they will be out exploring.

There is a gregarious energy to goldfinches. They have excellent flying skills and seem to have fun dipping and rising in wavelike patterns. Goldfinches are also social and can be found in large flocks of 40 to 100 birds, which are called "charms." Even when threatened by predators, goldfinches do not act aggressively but use sound as an alarm. Their sounds and songs are a series of musical warbles and twitters. Some bird-lovers have said the call of goldfinches sounds like they are saying, "po-ta-to-chip."

Seeds are the favorite food of goldfinches and their bodies have adapted to help them get what they love most. They use their feet to hang from seed heads in a position that can reach the seeds more easily. This dexterity enables goldfinches to take advantage of food sources relatively inaccessible to competitors. Their long and narrow beaks allow them to extract otherwise inaccessible seeds from thistles. These characteristics and more reduce the work of goldfinches have to do while simultaneously increasing their chances of survival.

Goldfinches are bright, energetic, and playful birds who add a sense of delight to their environment.

As a Head Type in the Positivity Triad, Type 7s are clarifying and synthesizing, like air, while also being migratory and contentment-focused like herbivores. Type 7s are bright with optimism and a zest for life. They fly above and around negative things by seeking out fun, exciting, and positive alternatives. Sometimes the needs of others can feel like a burden to them because Type 7s are focused on ways to get what they most want. Type 7s are social and gregarious and don't tend to be aggressive. Their coping strategy is to flee from a threatening internal world and seek security in the external world. When healthy, Type 7s bring social sensibilities and joy that can offer a lightness to conflict while still addressing the difficulties.

Reflection Questions for Type 7s:
When has my positivity and energy helped others find hope in times of conflict?
Are there times when I have avoided something difficult that was needed by moving instead towards something exciting that I wanted?
How can I bring brightness to those around me without overlooking the darkness?

Omnivores & The Competency Triad
Enneagram Types 1, 3, & 5

Omnivores are flexible eaters, consuming a variety of material based on availability. They can range from small creatures, like ants, to large ones, like bears. It takes strategy to compete with specialized eaters in environments where food is plentiful, so omnivores have to use their intelligence to search for, identify, and evaluate new sources of food.

There are biological adaptations that help omnivores eat a variety of foods. Their mouths often include both sharp teeth that can be used to cut meat and flat molars that can process plant material. This makes them the most adaptable eaters of the animal kingdom, giving them food security even during times of stress and scarcity. They survive difficult circumstances by adjusting their diets. Because of their varied diets, omnivores help control the size of animal populations and vegetation overgrowth.

During times of prolonged scarcity or need, omnivores can shift to eating like carnivores or herbivores for seasons or even years. Even as they do so, they are considered omnivores because it is not biology but strategy that is determining their eating patterns.

Omnivores are intelligent problem-solvers who can find provision wherever they are and balance the resources of their environments.

The Types in the Competency Triad are generally analytical in the face of difficulty, with a focus on solving problems. They use their brains to identify and evaluate negative situations, deciding strategically what to consume and what to avoid. In times of conflict, Competency Types are likely to suppress their feelings with the hope of remaining objective, effective, logical and competent. They are adaptive problem-solvers who have issues operating within systems that feel too restrictive. These Types rationalize action steps and distance from emotion. They want to be effective, calm, and controlled until there is resolution.

Reflection Questions for Types in the Competency Triad:
How has my competency and adaptability brought solutions to difficult situations?
When have I suppressed emotions and missed the relational sides of conflict?
What would it look like to balance analysis and effectiveness with vulnerability?

HOW WE REACT TO & COPE WITH THE WORLD

Bear
Enneagram Type 1

Bears systematically change what they eat based on seasons. During hibernation, their heart rate drops and their bodies release an appetite-suppressing hormone. When emerging from hibernation, they scavenge for the meat of animals that died during the winter. In spring, they take the opportunity to eat the tender sprouts of the newly growing plants. As bears move into summer and fall, they eat insect colonies and wild berries.

As they move through these seasons, bears take advantage of their impressive navigational abilities. As they move about their territories, they take an inventory of their surroundings and memorize a detailed map. They use these maps to track down their favorite foods, even if it has been years since they have seen it. Bears also use these navigational skills to cover their tracks or conceal themselves when they encounter a threat.

Along with these skills, bears also have strength, dexterity, and learning ability. They can turn over rocks three times their body weight when they are in danger or bored. They can swim and climb to get access to food sources like salmon or beehives. When bears do make it to a beehive at the top of a tree, they can use their paws to scrape honeycombs together to eat both the larvae and honey inside. All the while putting up with the stings for the reward of the sweetness. Bears who live near population centers have learned to open jars and manipulate door latches. In fact, when asked why it's hard to design a bear-proof garbage can, a Yosemite Park Ranger notably replied, "There is a considerable overlap between the intelligence of the smartest bears and the dumbest tourists."

Bears are determined and clever opportunists who demonstrate detailed memory and processing skills.

As a Gut Type in the Competency Triad, Type 1s are grounded and strong, like the earth, while also being analytical and solution-focused like omnivores. Type 1s are determined, sharp, and strong. Others can feel threatened by the strong presence of Type 1s. They use logic to find the "right" answer and if something goes wrong, work to figure it out in order to do better next time. Type 1s focus on solving problems. They do what is sensible, manage feelings and channel the energy of struggle into efficiency. Their coping strategy is to stay reasonable and logical, so difficulties can be improved according to their standards. When healthy, Type 1s bring an objective serenity into conflict that builds a path to sincere resolution.

Reflection Questions for Type 1s:
When has my objectivity brought resolution in times of conflict?
Are there times when I have repressed emotion and become critical or rigid?
How might I open space for solutions that include the needs of heart, mind, and body?

3

Lobster
Enneagram Type 3

Lobsters never stop growing and show no signs of aging. If a lobster loses a claw or leg, it grows it back. Since a lobster's shell does not change size, they shed their shells and grow new ones as they age. They consume the discarded shells after molting in order to replenish lost calcium and speed up the hardening of a new shell. Older lobsters continue to eat, have a stable metabolism, move with energy, and reproduce with vigor. After lobsters mate, the female carries the male's sperm for up to a few years in order to choose the optimal time and location to fertilize her eggs. Scientists consider lobsters to be biologically immortal.

There are small hairs on the legs and antennae of lobsters that sense and smell for food sources, making them capable of finding even microscopic proteins. Typically lobsters eat like carnivores, consuming clams, crabs, and small fish. But they are opportunistic eaters who also feed on aquatic plants when marine animals are scarce. In fact, when plants are also not available, lobsters become cannibals and feed on one another. Their focus is on their individual growth more than the well-being of their species.

Most humans have not seen the true color of a lobster. Lobsters in nature are a wide range of colors, including green, blue, yellow, gray, white, and multi-colored. When a lobster is cooked, only the red pigments in the shell are able to bear the heat, which results in the bright red shell most humans associate with them.

Lobsters have strategic and resourceful biological features that enable them to focus on growth throughout their lives.

As a Heart Type in the Competency Triad, Type 3s are nourishing and connective like water, while also being analytical and solution-focused like omnivores. Type 3s keep growing, honing their energy into problem-solving, goals, and accomplishments. They focus on getting what is needed to shed difficulties, letting go of what doesn't fit and rebuilding what does. Type 3s have a desire to be valuable and accepted, causing them to repress emotions and focus on tasks that will help them achieve their goals. Their coping strategy is to wear masks of success, not letting many people see their true colors. When healthy, Type 3s help communities move through and past conflict in ways that promote growth and regeneration.

Reflection Questions for Type 3s:
When has my strategy and forward momentum helped people move through conflict?
Are there times when I have focused on growth to the detriment of emotion or connection?
How can I take more time to feel the vulnerability of difficulties before moving forward?

5

Raven
Enneagram Type 5

Ravens are resourceful and calculating. They can use their beaks to rip objects, harness tools to obtain what they want, and push rocks onto people to keep them from finding their nests. Sometimes when there is a dead carcass, ravens will play dead next to it in order to scare others away. The diet of ravens varies based on habitat and available food sources. They hoard and hide their food to make sure they have enough. Furthermore, if a raven knows another raven is watching, it will pretend to hide its food in one place while really putting it in another.

In captivity, ravens can learn to talk better than some parrots. In the wild, they have been known to imitate wolves or foxes to attract them to carcasses that the raven isn't capable of breaking open. They are the only known bird to use signals and gestures to communicate, including holding up objects to get the attention of other birds. In Norse mythology, the god Odin had two ravens named Hugin ("thought") and Munin ("memory"), which flew around the world every day and reported back what they saw.

When a raven's friend loses in a fight, they seem to comfort the losing bird. They can also remember birds they like and will respond in a friendly way to certain birds for at least three years after seeing them. Ravens are generally monogamous, with some pairs even mating for life. At the same time, before beginning nesting or reproduction, ravens define their territory and defend it aggressively. When ravens form groups, the flock is called a "conspiracy."

Ravens are intelligent birds, who seem capable of connection while still being guarded.

As a Head Type in the Competency Triad, Type 5s are clarifying and synthesizing, like air, while also being analytical and solution-focused like omnivores. Type 5s like to detach and defend their territory, becoming confident experts. Focused on withdrawing from emotions, Type 5s fly over difficulties with thought and memory, using intellect to solve the problem. They desire to be capable and competent and will hoard resources and information, working independently to achieve the outcome they want. Their coping strategy is to withdraw and not rely on others to protect themselves from being let down. When healthy, Type 5s bring both insight and empathy into conflict, which come together to create thoughtful resolution.

Reflection Questions for Type 5s:
When has my thoughtfulness brought needed perspective to conflict?
Are there times when I have guarded my resources instead of sharing needed insights?
How can I be more fully present by bringing both my heart and my head to problems?

"One of the basic principles about the enneagram is that it charts universal truths about the nature of reality and the nature of human beings... While the issues and conundrums symbolized at each point of the enneagram are stronger for those of that type, they are issues and conundrums that we all share."

Sandra Maitri

How We Relate to & Provide for the World:
Plant Groupings & The Collaboration Triads

The complexity and distinctiveness of plant varieties makes them difficult to categorize— especially since botanists discover and study new flora every year. Plants, like any living thing, need to reproduce, and there are three different ways they do so. Spore-producing plants reproduce themselves independently by spreading spores. Rhizome-making plants expand through colonization, using underground stems that grow roots. Flower-bearing plants have stamens and pistils in their flowers that create seeds dispersed by wind or animals.

All three of these plant groupings are important for the functioning of the earth's ecosystems and all carry distinct features from one another. In the Enneagram system, the nine Types are divided into three distinct collaboration triads,* which describe how we relate to and provide for the world.

Types 8, 2, and 5 are in the Relationalist Triad. The Types in this Triad use their Intelligence Center Triad to provide necessary support for others. People rely on them as anchors. These Types offer themselves to the world, giving the strength and protection of their presence (Type 8s), providing the care and support of their relationship (Type 2s), or exhibiting the reason and perspective of their minds (Type 5s). This Triad is sometimes called the Rejection Triad because they tend to reject something essential in order to avoid rejection from others.

Types 9, 3, and 6 are in the Pragmatist Triad. The Types in this Triad use their Intelligence Center Triad to provide tangible support and down-to-earth effectiveness. People are attracted to the ways they offer stability. These Types look for ways to practically relate to the world, seeking a comfortable harmony (Type 9), fulfilling productive and ambitious roles (Type 3s), or finding a secure and predictable path (Type 6s). This Triad is sometimes called the Attachment Triad, as they demonstrate different forms of constructive connection.

Types 1, 4, and 7 are in the Idealist Triad. The Types in this Triad use their Intelligence Center Triad to provide perspective of what could be. People appreciate how they move towards what is possible. These Types seek ultimate ideals, pushing for high standards (Type 1s), dreaming of a reality where nothing is missing (Type 4s), or hoping for freedom from pain (Type 7s). This Triad is sometimes called the Frustration Triad because of the feeling that rises in them from all that doesn't match these visions.

The Relationalist Triad is like Spore-producing Plants, the Pragmatist Triad is like Rhizome-making plants, and the Idealist Triad is like Flower-bearing plants. Think about how different the world would be if any one of these plant groupings were missing. The same is true for humanity. These three different ways of relating to and providing for the world are each valuable. Each Triad offers something important for the flourishing of humanity.

*Belinda Gore calls these the Object-Relations Triads: Frustration (Types 1, 4, and 7), Rejection (Types 2, 5, and 8), and Attachment (Types 3, 6, and 9). Helen Palmer uses Flow (Types 1, 4, and 7), Power (Types 2, 5, and 8), and Blend (Types 3, 6, and 9). Dr. David Daniels uses the term Harmony Triads, with the same inner groupings as labeled above. I coined the term Collaboration Triads working with teams.

Spore-producing Plants & The Relationalist Triad
Enneagram Types 8, 2, & 5

Spore-bearing plants include horsetails, clubmoss, spikemoss, and ferns. These plants are distributed around the world in tropical, temperate, and boreal environments.

These plants reproduce asexually with spores that form on the underside of mature leaves and stems of a plant, looking like small dots on the fronds. In dry conditions, they separate from the leaves and are able to be dispersed by wind or water. Millions of spores may separate from plants, but only a few will find the conditions necessary to complete the lifecycle and grow. After separation, a spore becomes a gametophyte, which fertilizes into a zygote and eventually becomes a mature plant. Reproduction takes two generations to complete.

Cryptogams are another name for spore-bearing plants, because their means of reproduction is hidden. There are about 12,000 species of *cryptogams*, with the fern family making up 90% of the species diversity. Ferns are the oldest plants in the world, first appearing in the fossil record about 360 million years ago. They mostly are found in shady forests, crevices in rocks, acidic wetlands, or tropical trees. In each of these cases, there is something about the environment that would make other plants struggle, yet ferns thrive.

Spore-bearing plants are independently resourceful, needing little assistance to spread and expand what they have to offer.

The Types in the Relationalist Triad want to provide an important function for the world through offering something from themselves. They counter fears of rejection by contributing independently from their own resources, reproducing without help. This Triad protects itself from depending upon others by overcompensating with their gifts, offering themselves so that things will grow. They can hide in their contributions and not reveal their deeper needs. As Dr. David Daniels states, "The path for those of us leading with these types is to release the deeply held concern of being rejected and to open the heart to the natural flow of energy that is love and life itself."

Reflection Questions for Types in the Relationalist Triad:
How has my relationalist posture offered something to others that this world needed?
When has fear of rejection closed me to relational reciprocity?
How can I connect to the truth of my own needs and shift what I am offering accordingly?

8

Scaly Tree Fern
Enneagram Type 8

Scaly Tree Ferns, also known as Cyatheaceae, are a family of ferns that includes over 600 species. They can thrive in a variety of environments but are most often found in rainforests, growing alongside other canopy-height plants. Their height varies according to the species and growing conditions, with some reaching heights of over 60 feet. They have large, feathery fronds, which are divided into small leaflets. These fronds are massive, reaching 9 feet long or more. The bases of their fronds are covered in dark brown spines that are prickly to the touch.

Cyatheaceae is from the Greek word *kyatheion*, which means little cup. This name comes from the presence of a thin membrane coating that functions as a shield around the spores of this plant. Their other name, Scaly Tree Fern, comes from their coarse trunks that have circular marks left behind when they drop their fronds. These marks resemble reptile scales. Their trunks are not actually trunks like those on trees but a collection of dense stalks that provide support for the crown of fronds and a collection place for water and nutrients.

Individual plants can live for hundreds of years, and as a family, scaly tree ferns have been on this planet for more than 200 million years. Yet, most varieties are now under protection. Humans have over-collected the coverings from their trunks as a material for cultivating orchids. Plus, the rainforests they call home are threatened by climate change.

Scaly Tree Ferns are massive yet varied, strong yet vulnerable, and an important resource for cultivating life and beauty.

As a Gut Type in the Relationalist Triad, Type 8s are grounded and strong, like earth, while also offering themselves, like spore-bearing plants. Type 8s relate to the world with a towering strength and offer their protection to others. They are adapted to survive, shielding themselves and their future from harm. Though this makes them tough, it may also hinder them from seeing their true vulnerability. Sometimes they are prickly to the touch and can scare others away. When Type 8s trust that they need to receive protection even as they assert hardiness, they offer what is truly their best gift, the freshness of opening to life one day at a time.

Reflection Questions for Type 8s:
When has my towering strength provided important assertiveness to the world?
Are there times when I have shielded too much of myself and scared others away?
How can I let go of control and relate to others with more trust?

2

Scouring Horsetail
Enneagram Type 2

Scouring Horsetail plants form dense colonies in reliably wet environments, like wetlands, marshes, swamps, and river edges. They can tolerate flooding and live in up to four inches of standing water. Other names for it include rough horsetail, scouring rush, or snake grass. Its scientific name, *Equisetum Hyemale,* means, "horse bristles in winter" in Latin, perhaps because it is an evergreen in warmer climates. These plants can be found all over North America, Europe, and Northern Asia and date back to 350 million years ago.

At the nodes of scouring horsetail plants, tiny leaves clasp like teeth around ridges filled with silica. The cylindrical and segmented hollow stems reach three to five feet high, with what appears to be a cone at the top. That cone is not filled with seeds, as one might expect, but is actually covered with spores that help this plant spread. It grows easily, and can even become an invasive species.

Historically, these plants have been gathered and cultivated for a number of uses. The rough ridges of the stems have been used to scour and scrape pots, hence its name. In Japan, the stalks are dried to make a traditional fine-grade polishing material for metal. The stems can also be dried and shaped into reeds for woodwind instruments like clarinets and saxophones. Horsetail is also an ancient homeopathic treatment. Romans applied the silica in the stems topically to wounds in order to stop bleeding. Some Indigenous tribes boiled or dried the stalks, creating a remedy that could be ingested to function as a diuretic or strengthen bones.

Scouring horsetails are prolific growers that are useful to humanity for both help and healing.

As a Heart Type in the Relationalist Triad, Type 2s are nourishing and connective like water, while also offering themselves, like spore-bearing plants. Type 2s prefer environments reliably full of heart, providing community for themselves and others even when emotions flood their surroundings. They give of themselves generously, sometimes even invasively, as they build those connections. Type 2s offer what they have to others, wanting to give help, hope, and healing. Sometimes, they do not recognize how they have been uprooted from their own needs in the process and lost connection to the flow that provides for them. When Type 2s can support others without intruding and offer help without cutting themselves off from their own needs, they bring what is truly their best gift: altruistic humility.

Reflection Questions for Type 2s:
When have I provided healing and a sense of connection and belonging to the world?
Are there times when I have sacrificed myself in the process of supporting others?
How can I stay connected to the humble and benevolent flow of giving and receiving?

5

Bird's Nest Fern
Enneagram Type 5

Bird's Nest ferns are epiphytic plants, growing on branches and trunks of trees in rainforests worldwide. They like warmth and humidity but not direct sunlight, which is why they prefer the partial shade offered by their epiphytic perch. Their bright green fronds look a bit like banana leaves and, in the right conditions, can reach four to five feet long. New leaves emerge from the center and are fragile to the touch when young. Spores are produced in orderly brown parallel lines on the underside of the fronds. Their bright color, rosette shape, and need for little maintenance make Bird's Nest ferns popular houseplants. However, indoors they grow to only about half the size of what they reach in the wild.

Their fronds grow in a bowl shape, rolling back, turning brown, and creating a "nest" around the plant as they die. This nest shape helps these ferns trap both water and organic matter, providing them with needed nutrients and allowing them to be self-sufficient. Other living things like mosses and small animals take advantage of the resources stored by these ferns and grow in and around their shelter.

The scientific name is Asplenium Nidus. Asplenium means "without a spleen" in Latin, as Ancient Greeks believed it could cure spleen diseases. Nidus means nest, referring again to this fern's appearance. In the traditional medicine of Indigenous tribes, leaves were used to treat fever, relieve headaches, and ease labor pains.

Bird's Nest ferns are self-sufficient plants that provide for themselves and others through the way they grow.

As a Head Type in the Relationalist Triad, Type 5s are clarifying and synthesizing, like air, while also offering themselves, like spore-bearing plants. Type 5s grow best in environments where they can have the perspective of elevation and the protection of shelter. They store energy and ideas, offering independence to themselves and resources to others. Type 5s tend to grow slowly, wanting to relate to the world when they feel capable. They like the thoughts they produce to be orderly and sensical. Though this slowness can make Type 5s feel secure, ultimately they reject full connection to both themselves and others. When Type 5s open to the energy of risk, moving towards life, they offer the deeper wisdom of free-flowing energy.

Reflection Questions for Type 5s:
When has my ability to offer perspective and competence given insight to others?
Are there times when I have moved too slowly or held too much back?
How can I take the risk of moving towards others before I have things figured out?

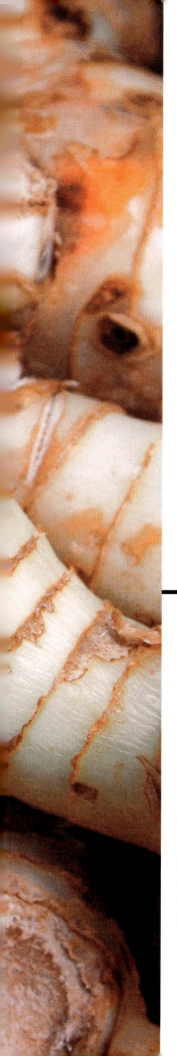

Rhizome-making Plants & The Pragmatist Triad
Enneagram Types 9, 3, & 6

Rhizome is Greek for "mass of roots." Though they look like roots, rhizomes are actually modified stems. There are nodes on these stems that produce both shoots and roots that are able to asexually reproduce the plant. Rhizomes grow both below and above ground, and in single or multiple layers. They are adaptable to what works best for each plant in each environment. This brings an efficiency to rhizome reproduction with the potential to spread too far or too fast and become an invasive species.

Nutrient storage inside of rhizomes makes them not only good for reproduction but also for providing energy. These gathered nutrients give these plants the needed resources to sprout new plants after dying back for the winter. Ginger and turmeric are two types of rhizomes that humans eat.

When plants have rhizomes, that is the easiest and best way to propagate them, even when there is the option of seeds or spores. After a rhizome is cut, each section that has a node can grow a new plant. These new plants are genetically identical to the parent plant. Technically, a group of plants connected through rhizomes are, in fact, a single organism.

Rhizomes are an efficient way for plants to both reproduce and have the nutrients they need for growth.

The Types in the Pragmatist Triad want to provide a practical productivity that keeps the world working. They rely on habitual ways of functioning, storing, and growing naturally alongside others. They are adaptable to their environments and the needs of those around them. This Triad also attaches to what works for them, which can mean an over-attachment to their own patterns. Sometimes, that looks like stored resources everyone can benefit from, and sometimes, that looks like expansion without thought. As Dr. David Daniels states, "The path for those of us with one of these three types is to release from reassuring worldly attachments as the way of being in the world. Allow in emotional discomfort (that challenges our relied-upon routines)."

Reflection Questions for Types in the Pragmatist Triad:
How has my pragmatism provided needed down-to-earth support for others?
When have I fallen into patterns and moved without thoughtfulness or intention?
How can I detach from comfort and routine while still growing with efficiency?

9

Quaking Aspen Tree
Enneagram Type 9

Quaking Aspen trees are native to North America and can be found from Alaska to Mexico. They are known for their trembling leaves, which have flexible stems that rotate easily in the wind. The leaves turn from a vibrant green in the summer to a brilliant yellow in the autumn. Many animals eat the leaves and bark of aspens, making them a keystone species because of how much of the surrounding ecosystem relies on them for survival.

Reaching heights of 50 feet or more, Quaking Aspens are fast growing. A chromosomal abnormality restricts many of these trees from being able to reproduce using flowers. Instead, aspens grow through rhizomes that extend hundreds of feet underground and sprout seedlings that are clones of the original tree. Those seedlings are reluctant to grow because of a hormone stored in the roots. That hormone is disrupted by wildfires, making fire a necessary component of their growth. Forest rangers have found as many as 40,000 Aspen seedlings growing per acre after a moderate wildfire.

Though they look like forests, many Quaking Aspen groves are actually a single organism. The rhizomatic reproduction interconnects all the trees below ground. One such aspen grove in Utah has been named Pando, which is Latin for "I spread." Pando is contains nearly 47,000 individual trees with the same DNA that cover 106 acres and weigh 12 million pounds, making it the biggest known organism in the world.

Quaking Aspens are resistant yet prolific growers, depending on one another's roots for stability and resources.

As a Gut Type in the Pragmatist Triad, Type 9s are grounded and strong, like earth, while also being practically productive like rhizome-making plants. Type 9s provide necessary support to their environment, and are relied on by many. Because the life they offer is more down-to-earth, or even below ground, sometimes the impact of their presence can be unseen or taken for granted. As a result, Type 9s can be reluctant to spread their influence, holding back from regeneration and growth. Though they avoid disruption, fire can in fact be the very thing they need to be released. When Type 9s can see the true magnitude of their presence, and the distinctive beauty of their movements in the world, they radiate loving action.

Reflection Questions for Type 9s:
When have others relied on me for pragmatic support and a stable presence?
Are there times when I have not recognized my own size, beauty, or importance?
How can I be less afraid of disruption, and relate to the world with the significance of my own presence?

3

Cyperus Papyrus
Enneagram Type 3

Cyperus Papyrus plants are tender yet vivacious aquatic plants that grow around lake and river edges in Africa, Madagascar, and the Mediterranean. With a preference for warm climates and wet conditions, they have slender stems that can grow to about 15 feet tall and are topped with clusters of white greenish-brown flowers. These stems grow from robust and woody rhizomes.

The flowering tops of Papyrus plants look like feather duster umbrellas, creating an ideal nesting site for many birds. The lightness of the flowers also allows for pollination to occur by wind. Since pollination is occurring at the same time as rhizomatic reproduction, Papyrus plants are fast-growing and wide-spreading.

The Ancient Egyptians made efficient use of all parts of Papyrus plants, which grew readily along the Nile River. The fiber inside the stems was used to make scrolls, allowing for the advancement of written language as early as 3000 BCE. The woody rhizomes were used for making bowls that would be burned for fuel after use. The stems were used to make sandals, baskets, and rope. Because the stems float, they were also used to make the boats and rafts depicted on ancient hieroglyphics. Though it was once prevalent in Egypt, the Cyperus Papyrus is now almost extinct along the Nile Delta. At the same time, it has become invasive in non-native habitats, disrupting waterways and threatening the growth of native species.

Cyperus Papyrus plants are fast-spreading, graceful, useful, and historically significant.

As a Heart Type in the Pragmatist Triad, Type 3s are nourishing and connective like water, while also being practically productive like rhizome-making plants. Type 3s provide efficient, useful, and significant support to their environment, often allowing for advancement that could not have happened without their gifts. They relate to the world with sustaining productivity, spreading what they have fast and wide. Sometimes, this can turn Type 3s into more of an invasive presence, if they take over and disrupt in the wrong places. It can also cause burnout, as Type 3s can give so much of themselves that they disappear. When Type 3s connect to the grace of their existence, not just their effectiveness, they offer an enduring hope to the world.

Reflection Questions for Type 3s:
When have others relied on my pragmatic productivity in order to move forward?
Are there times when I have pushed too hard and either exhausted others or myself?
How can I work with the hopeful energy of the beauty that already exists and the potential of what could be produced?

6

Queen's Tears Bromeliads
Enneagram Type 6

Queen's Tears is a species of epiphytic bromeliad plant native to Brazil, Argentina, Uruguay, and Paraguay. Like other epiphytes, they grow on trees but are not parasites, using the rocks or trees they grow on for support but not taking nutrients from them.

Billbergia Nutans, the scientific name of Queen's Tears Bromeliads, produce long, tough, leathery leaves with toothed edges. The leaves act as funnels to collect rain water and debris, which are absorbed through scales on their leaves. Their roots are used as anchors that fasten them to their hosts and are adaptable to become terrestrial if knocked to the ground. Queens Tear's stems arch towards the ground and hang with what appears to be pink flowers but are actually bracts, specialized leaves designed to protect the flowers from extreme conditions. At the base of the bracts dangle clusters of blue and green flowers with yellow stamens. Those stamens drip nectar when Queen's Tears are jostled, creating the appearance of crying and giving these plants their common name.

It takes until bromeliads are 2-3 years old before they begin producing flowers. Once they do, those flowers last for months. After the blooms are gone, the plant puts its energy into producing new shoots, called pups, through its rhizomes. As the mother plant fades, its pups grow. Though named pups, these small plants aren't children but clones of the original plant.

Queen's Tears plants are also called Friendship plants, as their propensity to produce multiple pups allow gardeners to easily propagate and spread their life to others.

As a Head Type in the Pragmatist Triad, Type 6s are clarifying and synthesizing, like air, while also being practically productive like rhizome-making plants. Type 6s understand how to collect the resources and create the adaptations necessary for survival. They protect what is delicate and look for support from others as they do so. If something cuts them off from that support, they will leave and find another way to persist. Type 6s take their time to bloom, wanting to ensure they have enough provision before they do so. They may struggle to hold the vulnerability of offering themselves in visible ways, becoming emotional or fearful when that tenderness is disturbed. When Type 6s connect to their inner support, they can bloom with more endurance and confidence, offering courage to the world.

Reflection Questions for Type 6s:
When has my ability to collect and manage resources offered needed care to others?
Are there times when I have waited too long to bloom because of fear?
How can I trust my own inner strength to flower, be vulnerable, and support others at the same time?

Flower-bearing Plants & The Idealist Triad
Enneagram Types 1, 4, & 7

Flower-bearing plants come in many forms and make up 90% of the plants on earth. The biodiversity of flower-bearing plants means they can be found almost anywhere, from deserts and forests to oceans and ponds. There are almost 350,000 different species of flower-bearing plants that have currently been discovered. Many are admired for their beauty.

The traits of flower-bearing plants can reveal how they are pollinated. The flowers of wind-pollinated plants are simple and often lack petals. These plants, including many trees and grasses, produce large amounts of pollen early in the growing season that can be dispersed before leaves get in the way.

The various features of creature-pollinated plants are more complex. In fact, Charles Darwin called the sudden explosion and diversification of flower-bearing plants in the fossil record an "abominable mystery." Scientists now know that it was the connection between flowering plants and pollinating insects that caused a co-evolution. Flower traits that attracted insects, (like color, shape, and scent) developed in plants, while features that improved pollination (like mouth and body shape) developed in insects. This co-evolutionary relationship led to the growth and expansion of both. Now, creatures that pollinate flower-bearing plants include not only insects but moths, birds, bats, and even lizards.

Life on earth is dependent on the nutrients produced by both flower-bearing plants and their pollinators.

The Types in the Idealist Triad want to provide a beautiful vision to the world by searching for their ideal. They relate to those around them in a spirit of co-evolution, hoping to better each other in ways that also make the world better. This Triad carries seeds of a utopia within them and can become frustrated when that future doesn't grow. They may also get frustrated when they feel the need to allure others to pollinate and spread that vision, instead of it just being carried by the wind. As Dr. David Daniels states, "The path for those of us leading with one of the Idealistic types is to see into the frustration as an inherent part of the gift that also seeks ideals." There is good yet to come but that does not negate the beauty that is already here.

Reflection Questions for Types in the Idealist Triad:
How has my idealism inspired others to improve their lives or this world?
When have I allowed my frustration to get in the way of relating to what is already good and beautiful around me?
How can I open myself to both the possibility of tomorrow and the essence of today?

1

Canada Red Chokecherry Tree
Enneagram Type 1

The Canada Red Chokecherry tree is small to medium-sized, typically growing around 20 feet tall. This tree is known for its distinctive red bark. The bark is smooth and shiny when the tree is young, but becomes rough and scaly as the tree ages. These hardy trees are tolerant of temperature shifts, able to thrive in poor soil, and resistant to pests and diseases. They grow fast and need minimal care to thrive.

A favorite of birds and butterflies, Canada Red Chokecherry trees are distinct because, unlike many other flowering trees, they do not need other compatible trees nearby in order to be pollinated. They are efficient and autonomous in their reproduction.

The straight trunks of Canada Red Chokecherry trees develop into arching branches and an evenly rounded crown. The shape of the tree is symmetrical and beautiful, even without the leaves and flowers. Their leaves begin bright green and turn reddish purple in the early summer. These trees produce clusters of fragrant white flowers in the spring, followed by small red-purple fruit in the summer. The berries of the Canada Red Chokecherry trees are edible, but the fruit is often bitter, and the seeds can be poisonous. But, once the work is done to take out the seeds and cook them, they make delicious jams, jellies, and baked goods.

Canada Red Chokecherry trees are resilient and independent producers.

As a Gut Type in the Idealist Triad, Type 1s are grounded and strong, like earth, while also being evolving seed-spreaders, like flower-bearing plants. Type 1s are enduring, having the self control to reach high standards even in difficult conditions. They work to have beauty in both their form and function, demonstrating goodness at all times. However, what begins as potential can grow into bitter fruit when Type 1s allow their frustration about unmet ideals become criticism or perfectionism. Their once smooth exterior can become rough, to themselves and others. At the same time, their reliability to display excellence season after season can truly inspire others. When Type 1s can open to the process of pruning and cooking, the world is able to admire their wholeness and taste the sweetness of their serenity.

Reflection Questions for Type 1s:
When has my reliable goodness provided a vision of higher standards for the world?
Are there times when my frustration has grown into bitter fruit?
How can I find more contentment in what is and let go of what should be?

4

Swamp Hibiscus
Enneagram Type 4

The Swamp Hibiscus is also known as the Red Texas Star Perennial Hibiscus, Scarlet Rose Mallow, or the Swamp Mallow. Growing as a perennial in the southeastern United States, it can reach over 6 feet tall and up to 4 feet wide. Adapted for bogs and swamps, this hibiscus grows well in cloudy water that would kill many other plants. Swamp Hibiscus plants are resilient, tolerating not only acidic soil but both high temperatures and humidity. They filter the dirt and excess minerals, making the area around them more viable for other creatures.

Swamp Hibiscus die back to the ground in winter but resprout in late spring. They wait to emerge until the soil temperatures are warm, remaining safely underground until the frost danger has passed before growing again. In the right conditions, these plants grow quickly.

The flowers of a Swamp Hibiscus are red and enormous, up to 8 inches in diameter. The petals form a five-pointed star shape with highly visible stamens and pistils in the center. These features make the Swamp Hibiscus attractive to bees, butterflies, and hummingbirds. While these plants bloom throughout the late summer, each flower lasts only about one day. These flowers are often harvested by humans and dried for teas and other uses. Since the petals are flavorful but also bitter, they often need to be paired with other herbs and flavors for balance.

Swamp Hibiscus plants bring bright beauty to muddy places, offering a picture of hope and resilience.

As a Heart Type in the Idealist Triad, Type 4s are nourishing and connective like water, while also being evolving seed-spreaders, like flower-bearing plants. Type 4s are adapted to grow well in muddy conditions, filtering the dirt so all can thrive. They love to display beauty in swampy areas others have avoided, attracting others as they do this work. Sometimes, they get stuck working to attract a rescuer. Type 4s can also have flowers that fade quickly, as they struggle with the long-term energy needed to live out ideals. After prolonged struggle, they may pull back and get lost, only emerging when it feels safe to try again. When Type 4s can open to the steady work of filtering and blooming, they can demonstrate the lovely balance of equanimity.

Reflection Questions for Type 4s:
When has my ability to bloom in difficult places given others the courage they needed to embrace struggle?
Are there times when I have used up my energy trying to attract an ideal rescuer?
How can I see the beauty I am already creating with my presence?

Epiphytic Orchid
Enneagram Type 7

Orchids are the largest of all flowering plant families, with over 25,000 known species, 70% of which are epiphytes. Epiphytic Orchids are usually found in the inner branches of large trees, below the rainforest canopy. Since epiphytes obtain nutrients and moisture from the air, rain, and other sources, these plants do best in trees with rough bark, as they can access the water that gets lodged within the crevices.

Living in treetops allows epiphytic orchids to both receive better light and to avoid the herbivores that live on the forest floor. However, because they are not rooted in the soil, they need creative ways to find both nutrients and support. Most have bulging stems called pseudobulbs that store nutrients, enabling them to sustain themselves through times of drought. Their roots are covered by a white velamen coating, which both protects the plant and provides a spongy surface that is efficient at absorption. These features allow Epiphytic Orchids to thrive through both wet and dry cycles.

The seeds of orchids are the smallest of any plants, about the size of specks of dust. There is a prolific energy to the production of these seeds, with several million in just one seed pod. The balloon-like coatings around the pods allow these seeds to be easily carried by the wind.

Epiphytic Orchids are innovative resource finders and producers, sought after for their delightful appearance and bright energy.

As a Head Type in the Idealist Triad, Type 7s are clarifying and synthesizing, like air, while also being evolving seed-spreaders, like flower-bearing plants. Type 7s are adapted to grow well above the ground, seeking the light that helps them bloom while avoiding dirt and pain. They search for nutrients around them and adapt to absorb as much as possible. Type 7s can get frustrated when they feel stuck and throw out millions of seeds of ideas, hoping to spread to more places. Sometimes, Type 7s may lack the groundedness to see the beauty of where they are, not just the future potential. When Type 7s can focus on presence, they show us what can bloom in everyday moments.

Reflection Questions for Type 7s:
When have I helped others to look up and see the beauty of new possibilities?
Are there times when I focused too much on future potential and missed the present moment?
How can I see the beauty and diversity that exists in us already, right at this moment?

"The Enneagram is a sacred system, one that has passed through centuries and generations, evolving over time and offering greater and greater clarity about ourselves, others, processes , and consciousness at an individual and a collective level."

Ginger Lapid-Bogda

Conclusion

Pulling It All Together

Notice what rose to the surface for you as you journeyed through this book. *What Type(s) spoke to you? What was beautiful about your Type or another type that you haven't noticed before? What image spoke to you the most? Have you gotten out of the box and into the wild to discover new images where you live?*

Now that we have journeyed through all the layers, we can deepen this imagery through connecting them. Enneagram Triads give us a beautiful opportunity to see how we are unique and complex individuals while, at the same time deeply connected to each of the other Enneagram Types. Notice how each Enneagram Type can be described according to the Triadic layers. *Does this bring clarity to how you see yourself or someone else?*

- Type 8s are relational, reactive, active gut intelligence types.
- Type 9s are pragmatic, positive, receptive gut intelligence types.
- Type 1s are idealistic, competent, balancing gut intelligence types.
- Type 2s are relational, positive, balancing heart intelligence types.
- Type 3s are pragmatic, competent, active heart intelligence types.
- Type 4s are idealistic, reactive, receptive heart intelligence types.
- Type 5s are relational, competent, receptive head intelligence types.
- Type 6s are pragmatic, reactive, balancing head intelligence types.
- Type 7s are idealistic, positive, active head intelligence types.

In my work with teams, these Triadic connections have gone a long way to explain both sweet spots of collaboration and consistent points of tension.

What can be especially enlightening is to notice how our view expands when we keep the wisdom of the Intelligence Center Triads running throughout the other Triads, which has been done through these images. Every gut Type remains connected to the earth in all other Triadic imagery. Every heart Type remains connected to water in all other Triadic imagery. Every head Type remains connected to air in all other Triadic imagery. *How does that keep Types interconnected? How does it make Types distinct?*

Use the following pages for meditation and reflection. *How have you put yourself or others into boxes? How can you journey into the wild with these new images? Is there something present in these collage images that you haven't noticed before?*

Let's take the Enneagram journey further *into the wild* and see what we discover.

9

2

3

3

5

6

7

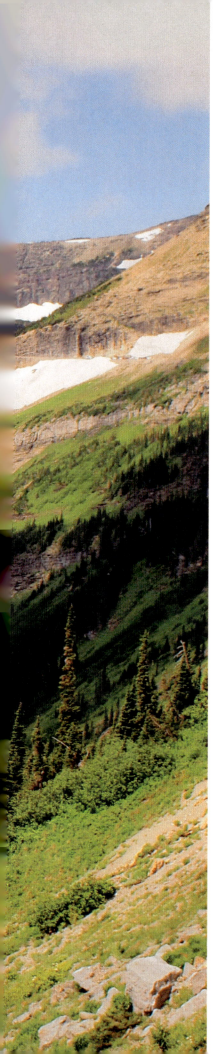

Closing Reflection

I hope this book has felt like a spacious exploration you can return to again and again. It is designed to be a companion on your Enneagram journey, providing a different view on who we are and why we do what we do. As we close, a blessing.

May you observe yourself
Without judgment
And without shame,
Holding compassion
For both who you have been
And who you are still becoming.

May you have eyes to see
The glorious wonders of who you are
Inherently
While simultaneously opening to
The innate goodness of others.

May you have the courage
To push against old patterns,
Release old biases,
Move in renewed ways,
And journey towards a fuller wholeness
Of what it is to live as you.

May you discover in the world around you
New imagery to guide you
And hold you
As you awaken to this truer
And deeper self.

May you understand
Just how essential
All of us
And each of us are,
Including you,
Especially you,
In the ecosystems
Of human community.

Appendices

Traditional Enneagram Terminology

The Enneagram is crowd-sourced and historical wisdom, which means its terminology is not copyrighted or controlled. Words vary from teacher to teacher. This can create new pathways for understanding but it can also be confusing. Below is some traditional and alternative terminology for Types and Triads:

Type	Passion	Virtue	Fixation	Essence
Type 1	Anger	Serenity	Resentment	Perfection
Type 2	Pride	Humility	Flattery	Freedom
Type 3	Deceit	Honesty	Vanity	Hope
Type 4	Envy	Equanimity	Melancholy	Origin
Type 5	Avarice	Non-Attachment	Stinginess	Omniscience
Type 6	Fear	Courage	Doubt	Faith
Type 7	Gluttony	Sobriety	Planning	Work
Type 8	Lust	Innocence	Vengeance	Truth
Type 9	Sloth	Action	Indolence	Love

Triad Terminology Used in this Book	Triad Terminology Used Elsewhere
Intelligence Center Triads	Sometimes simply referred to as "The Centers" Body or somatic sometimes used instead of Gut.
Energy Triads	Riso and Hudson apply the work of psychoanalyst Karen Horney and use the terminology "Hornovenian Groups." In that case, the Triads are categorized as Assertive, Withdrawing, and Compliant Types. Assertive is sometimes labeled as Aggressive, and Compliant is sometimes labeled as Dependent. Suzanne Stabile calls these Triads the Social Stances.
Harmonic Triads	Dr. David Daniels calls these the Emotional Regulation Triads, with the labels of Sustaining-Expressing (Types 8, 4, and 6), Reframing-Shifting (Types 9, 2, and 7), and Containing-Rationale (Types 1, 3, and 5). Positive Outlook is sometimes used instead of positivity.
Collaboration Triads	Belinda Gore calls these the Object-Relations Triads, with the labels of Frustration (Types 1, 4, and 7), Rejection (Types 2, 5, and 8), and Attachment (Types 3, 6, and 9). Helen Palmer uses the labels of Flow (Types 1, 4, and 7), Power (Types 2, 5, and 8), and Blend (Types 3, 6, and 9). Dr. David Daniel's uses the terminology of Harmony Triads, with the same inner groupings as labeled above.

Recommended Resources

Enneagram is a complex, rich, and beautiful tool that can take a lifetime of exploration and discovery. Here are some of my favorite resources.

Podcasts
- Enneagram 2.0 with Beatrice Chestnut and Uranio Paes
- The Art of Growth with Joel Hubbrad and Jim Zartman
- Do It for the Gram with Milton Steward
- Fathoms: An Enneagram Podcast with Seth Abram and Drew Moser
- Enneagram & Coffee with Sarajane Case

Websites
- integrative9.com
- enneagraminstitute.com
- enneagramworldwide.com
- drdaviddaniels.com (especially his article on harmony triads)

Books
- *The Enneagram Guide to Waking Up* by Beatrice Chestnut and Uranio Paes
- *The Path Between Us: An Enneagram Journey to Healthy Relationships* by Suzanne Stabile
- *Nine Lenses on the World* by Jerome Wagner
- *The Wisdom of the Enneagram* by Don Riso and Russ Hudson
- *Bringing Out the Best in Yourself at Work* by Ginger Lapid-Bogda
- *The Spiritual Dimension of the Enneagram* by Sandra Maitri
- *Roaming Free Inside the Cage: A Daoist Approach to the Enneagram and Spiritual Transformation* by William M. Schafer

Music
- Atlas: Enneagram (Songs written for each Enneagram Type) by Sleeping at Last

Organizations
- The Enneagram in Business
- The Narrative Enneagram
- Enneagram Minnesota
- The International Enneagram Association

Photo Credits

I (Stephanie J Spencer, author) am photographer for all images not listed below, including cover, introduction, and quote pages. Though I designed the other images, I cannot take credit for the photography itself. Much gratitude to all the artists of the world who share their talents so generously.

How We Perceive and Process the World: Intelligence Center Triads and The Elements
- Earth: Ray Bilcliff from Pexels
  - Rock: Renphoto from Getty Images Signature
  - Soil: StockSnap from Pixabay
  - Clay: vaitekune from Getty Images
- Water: Christos from Pexels
  - River: Nejron on Canva
  - Wave: shannonstent from Getty Images Signature
  - Iceberg: Photocreo
- Sky: Snapwire from Pexels
  - Wind: galdzer from Getty Images
  - Clouds: MagdaEhlers from Pexels
  - Rainbow: ThuyHaBich from pixabay

How we move and get our needs met in the world: Climate Zones and the Energy Triads
- Tropical: TISHA85 from Getty Images Pro
  - Mount Merapi: Mass Peot from Getty Images
  - Great Barrier Reef: Greg Sullavan from Getty Images
  - Hurricane: WikiImages from Pixabay
- Boreal: Eerik from Getty Images Signature
  - Norwegian Fjords: TOMAg from Getty Images
  - Lake Baikal: Ukususha from Getty Images
  - Aurora Borealis: Valdemaras D. from Pexels
- Temperate: Valiphotos from Pexels
  - North American Prairie: GracedByTheLight from Getty Images Pro
  - Merced Wildlife Refuge: Spondilolithesis from Getty Images Signature
  - Autumn (Harvest Moon): MelodyanneM from Getty Images

How we react to and cope with the world: Animal Groupings and the Harmonic Triads
- Carnivore: (lions) Tsepova_Ekaterina from Getty Images
  - Cheetah: Marcel Brekelmans from Getty Images Pro
  - Octopus: Freder from Getty Images Signature
  - Burrowing Owls: randimal from Getty Images
- Herbivore: (horses) Fotoneurotic from Getty Images
  - Elephants: Kamchatka on Canva
  - Beaver: Jillian Cooper from Getty Images
  - Goldfinch: Zhizia Shi from Getty Images
- Omnivore: (racoons) Jorge Figueiredo from Getty Images
  - Bear: Jupiterimages from Photo Images
  - Lobster: Janez_Kranjc from Getty Images
  - Raven: Piotr Krzeslak from Getty Images

How we relate to and provide for the world: Plant Groupings and the Collaboration Triads
- Spores: andipantz from Getty Images Signature
    - Scaly Tree Fern: imv from Getty Images Signature
    - Scouring Horsetail: Imágenes de oiasson on Canva
    - Bird's Nest Fern: photonewman from Getty Images
- Rhizome: studio2013 from Getty Images
    - Quaking Aspen: tntemerson from Getty Images
    - Cyperus Papyrus: weisschr from Getty Images
    - Queen's Tears Bromeliad: Julio Rivalta from Getty Images
- Flowering: ransirimal from Getty Images
    - Canada Red Chokecherry: Dee Carpenter Photography from Getty Images
    - Swamp Hibiscus: LagunaticPhoto from Getty Images
    - Epiphytic Orchid: seagames50 from Getty Images

Scientific Information Sources

The scientific information about each nature image was sourced from a combination of my own knowledge and internet research. Websites utilized include but are not limited to wikipedia.org, gardeningknowhow.com, thespruce.com, britannica.com, science.org, sciencedirect.com, education.nationalgeographic.org, exploringnature.org, fws.gov, rmg.co.uk, fjordnorway.com, barrierreef.org, and dw.com.

Acknowledgments

Any book is a group effort beyond the work of an author. I'm grateful.

To Robin Wall Kimmerer, whose book *Braiding Sweetgrass* opened my eyes to see the importance of our connection to nature. Your work sparked something deep within me for which I am grateful.

To the Enneagram teachers who have come before me, thank you for sharing this wisdom. The world owes you a debt of gratitude, and I do as well. Thank you especially to Jerome Wagner, Russ Hudson, Beatrice Chestnut, Uranio Paes, and Ginger-Lapid Bogda who have led me in trainings and workshops that have deepened my understanding of Enneagram beyond what books could have done.

To my Enneagram coaching clients who have helped me see what Enneagram Types look like embodied and lived out. Each one of you have helped me take Enneagram out of a box. I could hear your stories and think of your experiences as I wrote, and they pushed me to be careful and expansive in my language and images. Without you, this book would have been much more shallow and flat.

To Beth Graybill whose editing took my words and made them better. Not only that, you were the connection point to the publishing world that helped me feel like it could actually happen. So much of this book would not be what it is without your wisdom, support, and friendship.

To the folks at Punchline Publishing who held my hand through all the work that it is to take something from a manuscript to a published work. Joy and Amelia, thank you for giving me deadlines, goals, and clarity about how to manage this process. This Enneagram Type 4 would have been lost without the guidance your structure provided.

To David Kludt, Kirk Dunbar, Jim Fisher, Nicole Buehler, Cameron Spencer, Alex Spencer, and more who edited and proofread my words. Thank you for making this book better!

To friends who put up with my busy schedule and gave me feedback along the way. Thank you to Sara, Lisa, Alicia, Nicole, Jill, and others who offered encouragement, ideas, spaciousness, and honesty when I needed it.

To Kirk who made space for the disruption this book brought into our lives, and only rolled your eyes a little bit when I was down in my office yet again to get more done. The steady rock of your presence and the loving push for me to keep boundaries helped this book to come to life without killing me in the process.

To Cameron and Alex who make me proud every day just by being you. Thank you for helping behind the scenes with the tasks it took to get this done. I am grateful that I get to be your mom, and hold your stories in my heart when I create. I hope it inspires you to take risks and work hard to make your dreams reality.

Made in the USA
Monee, IL
17 June 2023

36010029R10095